PROVE ALL THINGS

PROVE ALL THINGS

The Sovereign Work of the Holy Spirit

D. MARTYN LLOYD-JONES

Edited by Christopher Catherwood

KINGSWAY PUBLICATIONS
EASTBOURNE

First published 1985

ISBN 0 86065 369 2

RV = Revised Version

Front cover design by Vic Mitchell

Printed in Great Britain for
KINGSWAY PUBLICATIONS LTD
Lottbridge Drove, Eastbourne, E. Sussex BN23 6NT by
Richard Clay (The Chaucer Press) Ltd, Bungay, Suffolk
Typeset by CST, Eastbourne, E. Sussex

Contents

Acknowledgements

The task of editing the manuscripts of both this book and the previous volume, *Joy Unspeakable*, would not have been possible without the help of my grandmother, Mrs Bethan Lloyd-Jones, and my mother, Elizabeth Catherwood, the Doctor's elder daughter. In many chapters the bulk of the editorial work had been carried out already by my grandfather Dr Martyn Lloyd-Jones before he died in 1981, as he fully intended these sermons to be published. All the other alterations were therefore essentially minor and of the type carried out in preparing the other series, such as those on Romans and Ephesians, where sermon material was turned into book form. I would therefore like to thank them for all the hours of hard work that they have put into *Joy Unspeakable* and *Prove All Things*.

CHRISTOPHER CATHERWOOD
Editor

John answered them, saying, I baptize with water: but there standeth one among you, whom ye know not. . . . And I knew him not: but he that sent me to baptize with water, the same said unto me, Upon whom thou shalt see the Spirit descending, and remaining on him, the same is which baptizeth with the Holy Ghost.

John 1:26, 33

Prove all things; hold fast that which is good.

1 Thessalonians 5:21

Tape Cassettes

Over 1600 tape cassettes of Dr Lloyd-Jones' sermons are to be made available by the Lloyd-Jones Recordings Trust, Crink House, Barcombe Mills, Near Lewes, East Sussex BN8 5BJ. A catalogue of the first 500 sermons published by the trust is now available. Four albums (24 cassettes in all) are available on 'The Baptism and Gifts of the Holy Spirit'—these form the substance of this book and *Joy Unspeakable*. Two albums of 12 cassettes on Revival (Revival 1 and Revival 2) are also available, as are other special albums.

Foreword

Dr Lloyd-Jones' pastoral preaching at Westminster Chapel was attuned to current spiritual needs as he saw them. So for twenty years he concentrated on correcting the anti-intellectualism of pious folk who would not use their minds to grasp God's truth, work out its application, and challenge falsehood in God's name. Then in the 1960s he found himself called to guide three sorts of people together: some who, having half-understood his earlier emphasis, were now becalmed in a biblicist 'orthodoxism' divorced from any real Christian experience; Calvinistic pietists, drawn to Westminster Chapel, who lacked assurance and joy; and feeling-oriented evangelicals who, having evaded the thrust of his earlier ministry, were now going overboard on charismatic concerns. As a good physician of the soul, diagnosing spiritual malaise in the light of the biblical understanding of spiritual health, Dr Lloyd-Jones saw the first group as moribund, the second as suffering from the spiritual equivalent of worms, and the third as vulnerable to cancerous fanaticism. The messages that make up this book are therapy for all three.

The quality of the preacher's presentation—his pastoral wisdom and didactic clarity, the vigour and rigour of his biblical thinking, the radiant and devastating intelligence of his arguments, and above all his pervasive passion for the honour of Jesus Christ and the health of the church—needs no commendation from me. I had better come clean and admit that I have reservations about the analysis of Spirit-baptism as a particular experience of assurance, which the opening section of this book assumes: it seems to me that Spirit-baptism on its experiential side should rather be defined in a broad way, as initiation into post-pentecostal Christian experience as such, with assurance of oneness with Christ in God's paternal love as one element of that. It must be right to urge, as Dr Lloyd-Jones does, that intense awareness of this oneness and love is a gift to be sought by prayer, but it is less certainly right to make this intensity of experience the whole substance of Spirit-baptism. For the main theses, however, of the present book, I have nothing but gratitude—that Spirit-baptism, though transforming in its effects, is not always marked by tongues, or by any other particular gift; that you cannot affirm that any spiritual gift has been permanently withdrawn; that the tongues of Acts 2 and of 1 Corinthians differ, though both are ecstatic in the same sense; that fanaticism is always self-oriented in some way; and others. These assertions seem to me incontrovertibly true, wise, and helpful amid the cross-currents of present-day debate. May the quickening of the church, for the sake of which Dr Lloyd-Jones preached all of this twenty years ago, be furthered by its publication now.

J. I. Packer

Introduction

In a churchyard in the middle of Welsh Wales, outside the town of Newcastle Emlyn, in the Teifi Valley, lies a simple grave. On it are inscribed the words 'Martyn Lloyd-Jones 1899–1981: "For I determined not to know anything among you save Jesus Christ and him crucified."' The church nearby had once been that of Evan Phillips, his wife Bethan's grandfather. It had seen revival—the great outpouring of the Holy Spirit with power—in the famous Welsh Revival of 1904–5. It seemed appropriate that my grandfather should have chosen to be buried there, because it had such a close link with the passion that he held throughout his ministry—that of revival, a visitation of the Holy Spirit upon the people of God, the church. From his study of Scripture he felt that it was only if people were baptized with the Holy Spirit, as in the book of Acts, that the power of the message of Jesus Christ crucified would be seen in the land.

'Phenomena,' my grandfather once told a group of doctors, 'must never determine belief.' One should only believe what Scripture clearly taught, and examine all unusual occurrences in its light. 'Be open,' he would say, 'be ready to listen, but never uncritical'—or, as the Apostle Paul put it, 'Prove all things; hold fast to that which is good'

(1 Thess 5:21). This book is therefore called *Prove All Things*. It is part of the series on the Holy Spirit that Dr Lloyd-Jones preached in Westminster Chapel, and chronologically it comes in the middle. It is a vital part of his teaching on the subject, and balances those sermons that form the earlier volume, *Joy Unspeakable*, published in 1984. As will soon become apparent, although my grandfather discusses the gifts of the Holy Spirit, this is not a book on the gifts as such. It is rather a biblical analysis of the results of baptism with the Holy Spirit with certain of the gifts being referred to along the way.

'There are many people,' my grandfather states, 'who reject the doctrine of the baptism because they reject the gifts.' It is precisely a desire to safeguard what he felt to be the Bible's teaching on baptism with the Holy Spirit that prompted my grandfather to introduce sermons on testing the spirits and proving all things.

Because he always started with the Scripture, rather than with subjective experience, my grandfather was naturally worried by what he felt were excesses that had grown up in the church, which followed on from a lack of biblical perspective. As he pointed out, 'It behoves us as Christian people to clarify our minds, to seek a true understanding in the light of scriptural teaching . . . and let us pray God to give us the spirit of understanding that we may lay hold of these things which clearly are difficult.' The church, he taught again and again, needed to be baptized with the Holy Spirit in the biblical sense of the term. The whole issue was 'one of the most urgent matters at this hour'. Yet there was confusion and division. The matter had to be examined, and, being the man he was, my grandfather did 'not believe in short cuts or glib answers—they are never satisfactory'.

What this book shows is that the Doctor held, as in all things, to a biblical balance and sense of proportion. On the one hand, he felt that to say that all the gifts had ceased with the end of the apostolic era was 'nonsense'. 'The Scriptures never anywhere say that these things were only temporary — never!' On the other hand, 'All these gifts . . . are under the sovereignty of the Spirit. He decides when and how and where.' So often Christians either quenched the Spirit or showed an 'uncritical acceptance of everything'. The simple, biblical fact of the matter was that 'the gifts of the Spirit are to be left in the hands of the Holy Spirit himself and it is he alone who decides'.

Furthermore, to bring us back to where we started, my grandfather firmly believed from Scripture that 'the baptism of the Spirit may itself be present in great power and yet none of these gifts may be manifest as such'. As he makes clear in *Joy Unspeakable*, the whole purpose of baptism with the Holy Spirit is to make us witnesses of Jesus Christ, in a time and place that has forgotten the message of the cross. The Holy Spirit is sovereign, and is sent not to draw attention to himself, but to make Jesus Christ central in all our lives. This is clear not only from Scripture itself, but again and again from the history of the Christian church.

'Jesus Christ and him crucified' was the great theme of my grandfather's life. It was why he regarded this issue of baptism with the Holy Spirit as so important—so that all may know of the glorious message of salvation. This is also why he was so anxious to safeguard the doctrine as he saw it, and why he was concerned that Christians test or 'prove' all things from Scripture. Tragically, today Christians are often more concerned with fighting each other, including over issues such as the gifts of the Holy Spirit, than seeking to win and save the lost with the gospel of Jesus Christ.

Whatever we may think the Bible's phrase 'baptism with the Holy Spirit' actually means—whether we agree with the interpretation given by my grandfather in *Joy Unspeak-*

able and here in *Prove All Things* or not—we should never forget that at the very heart of our message are the words on that tombstone in Wales: 'Jesus Christ and him crucified'.

CHRISTOPHER CATHERWOOD

Chapter I

Gifts that Authenticate

The words to which I should like to call your attention are to be found in John I: 26, 33—'John answered them, saying, I baptize with water: but there standeth one among you, whom ye know not . . . . And I knew him not: but he that sent me to baptize with water, the same said unto me, 'Upon whom thou shalt see the Spirit descending, and remaining on him, the same is he which baptizeth with the Holy Ghost.'

The subject we are dealing with is this great matter of the baptism with the Holy Spirit. I am trying to show that this is what enables us as Christian people to represent our blessed Lord and Saviour, and God our Everlasting Father, in this world of sin and shame.* We believe that this gospel of salvation is the supreme need of the world today, the supreme need of every individual, the only hope for the world at large. We are living in a world which is full of trouble and confusion; a world which has been trying to deal with and to solve its own problems throughout the centuries, and which is no nearer to solving them now than it was at the begin-

* See also *Joy Unspeakable*, the companion volume which discusses fully the baptism with the Holy Spirit.

ning; a world which, we believe, according to the teaching of Scripture, is under the wrath of God; a world which has turned away from God and brought down calamity and trouble upon itself; the only hope for such a world is in the gospel. And Christians are people who are called to be representatives of God's kingdom in that world. Endless statements to that effect can be found everywhere in the Bible.

The children of Israel, the Jews, were God's people and they were given the oracles of God. God gave the revelation to them in order that they might represent him before the nations of the world. And that is true of the Christian today; this is the business of the church, to tell the world as it is of this great and glorious salvation which is in Christ Jesus. He is the only hope of the world. There is no hope in men. The only hope is in the Son of God, and our business is to represent him, to glorify him among the people of the world, to magnify his name, to show them the excellencies of his person and of his great salvation; that is our business, we alone do that in this world. The church is to preach Christ, and him crucified, as the only hope, the only Saviour of the world; to declare that 'there is none other name under heaven given among men, whereby we must be saved' (Acts 4:12), and Christian people alone have that message, and they alone can present it to the world. The world does not know this message, it does not believe—that is the cause of its trouble. So we are called uniquely to bear witness to Jesus Christ and to magnify him.

But the question is: how can we do that? We are aware of the facts concerning him but he himself has taught that that is not sufficient. Christ tells even those trained apostles, his disciples who had been with him throughout his earthly ministry and had seen his death and burial, and were witnesses of his resurrection with their naked eyes, he tells them: 'Tarry ye in the city of Jerusalem until ye be endued with power from on high' (Lk 24:49). And on the day of Pentecost he sent that power upon them in a baptism of the Holy Spirit. And so we are trying to show that the central, main object of the baptism with the Holy Spirit is to enable us with the power to be witnesses to the Lord Jesus Christ, to his person, and to his work. And therefore there is nothing more important at the present hour than that we should understand this teaching.

We shall now spend some time considering what are the evidences of this baptism with the Spirit. I have divided them into two main categories: those which are more or less internal and subjective, known mainly to the man or woman himself or herself; and those which are more objective in their character and therefore visible to others. Obviously the objective evidences of the baptism are of vital importance in this whole matter of witness and of testimony.

One of the objective results of the baptism with the Spirit is at times seen even in a person's facial appearance, a kind of transfiguration, some reflection of the glory of God. As the face of Moses shone when he came down from the mountain having been with God, so there is something of this in the Christian. 'We all,' says Paul in 2 Corinthians 3:18, 'with open face beholding as in a glass the glory of the Lord, are changed into the same image from glory to glory, even as by the Spirit of the Lord.'

Let us next consider the evidence of the baptism with the Spirit as it shows itself in speech. The first great characteristic here is the power and the ability that is given not only in preaching but in ordinary conversation and in prayer. There are still people, I find, who seem to think that what we are talking about is only for certain special people. Now, that is a complete fallacy, for the New Testament offers this to all, and indicates clearly that this is possible to all. We must be clear about this. This baptism is not only for certain special people, and the Bible gives no such teaching. 'For the promise is unto you, and to your children, and to all that are afar off' (Acts 2:39). There are many illustrations, as we have seen, which show that ordinary unknown people can know this glorious experience in the same way as outstanding and distinguished people can. The devil would rob us of the most glorious aspects of the Christian faith. Let us therefore concentrate with all our powers as we study this together, lest he rob us of something that God is offering to us.

A further evidence of this baptism is the note of authority. Now this, of course, was the thing that struck people about our blessed Lord himself, though he was a carpenter and though he was, as judged by the world, a mere nobody. Yet when he began to speak they were struck at once by the way in which his teaching differed from that of the Pharisees and scribes. They said, 'This man speaketh and teacheth with authority, not as the Pharisees and scribes', and that was the great characteristic of his ministry.

But, do not forget, even the Lord, the Son of God incarnate, was not able to commence his ministry until he had been baptized with the Spirit at his baptism with water in the Jordan by John the Baptist. That is why the apostle John puts it here. John the Baptist had been told: 'He that sent me to baptize with water, the same said unto me, Upon whom thou shalt see the Spirit descending, and remaining on him, the same is he which baptizeth with the Holy Ghost' (Jn 1:33). And you remember what our Lord did when he went back after that to his home town of Nazareth, and went into the synagogue on the Sabbath day. He was given the Book to read and he began to speak. The passage which he read was that famous passage from Isaiah 61: 'The Spirit of the Lord God is upon me; because the Lord hath anointed me to preach good tidings unto the meek.' The anointing took place when the Holy Spirit descended upon him in the form of a dove at his baptism in the Jordan, and from that moment this authority appeared and it was evident to all.

This authority is something that was equally clear and evident in the apostles after their baptism with the Spirit. The contrast in the case of Peter is so striking. Read his sermon on the day of Pentecost, as recorded in Acts 2, and you are struck by the authority with which he spoke and taught that congregation and expounded the scriptures. There was no hesitation, no fumbling; yet this is the same man who, with the other disciples, could not at first even believe the report about the resurrection. Read the last chapter of Luke's gospel and you will find that when the women who had gone early to the tomb came back and reported to these very disciples the fact that they had found that tomb to be empty, they met with this reaction: 'Their words seemed to them as idle tales, and they believed them not' (Lk 24:11). The apostles were clearly muddled in their whole understanding of the Old Testament scriptures. But here is one of those men now speaking and expounding the scriptures with authority. This is always one of the results of the baptism with the Spirit.

And you get exactly the same thing in the case of the apostle Paul. There are such endless examples of this that one scarcely knows which to select. Let me give you one example from Acts 13 concerning the apostle Paul, on his first missionary journey in Cyprus. Paul began to preach and the chief man of the island was listening to him, but he had another man with him called 'Elymas the sorcerer'. Sergius Paulus, a prudent man, the governor, was very ready to listen, 'But Elymas the sorcerer withstood them, seeking to turn away the deputy from the faith. Then Saul, (who also is called Paul), filled with the Holy Ghost' (Acts 13:8-9). Now that was something that happened at that moment to him. It does not mean that he was always so filled with the Holy

Spirit. He was given special authority and power.

You find that being repeated right through the book of Acts. We are told of the disciples and others that they were 'filled with the Spirit' on the day of Pentecost. Then in chapter 4 Peter and John were on trial and had been commanded 'not to speak at all nor teach in the name of Jesus' (Acts 4:18). Threatened with extermination, they went back and they prayed to God, and God again sent the Spirit upon them, and they were filled again. And in the passage in Acts 13 Paul was given a special filling, another baptism, if you like, of power and authority. So you read this (verses 9-11): 'Then Saul, (who is also called Paul), filled with the Holy Ghost, set his eyes on him, And said, O full of all subtilty and all mischief, thou child of the devil, thou enemy of all righteousness, wilt thou not cease to pervert the right ways of the Lord? And now, behold, the hand of the Lord is upon thee, and thou shalt be blind, not seeing the sun for a season. And immediately there fell on him a mist and a darkness; and he went about seeking some to lead him by the hand.'

Now there, you see, is the authority, there is no hesitation. The Apostle knew. And all these men always knew. They had this authority in speech, they had this authority in performing miracles: it is always a characteristic. And as you read again the subsequent history of the church you will find that this authority invariably characterizes these people. You get it in every revival, you get it in great reformations. What was it that enabled Martin Luther to stand alone—alone against fifteen centuries of tradition with all the ecclesiastics against him? To stand alone and say, 'Here I stand, I can do no other, so help me God'? That is authority, and it has always characterized men who have received the baptism of the Spirit. And this is true not only in public declaration; the same assurance is evident in all people who know this experience.

The last thing I mention under this heading of objective evidence is boldness and fearlessness. This is very striking, and is again seen perhaps most perfectly in the instance of the apostle Peter himself. Peter was by nature a very impulsive man. He had a kind of boldness, too, but it was a natural boldness with a good deal of the braggart in it. When our Lord was taken captive and set on trial, and a serving maid recognized Peter and said, 'You were one of them; you were with this Galilæan', Peter you remember denied him; he denied him three times.

Why did he do that? Well, he was afraid, he was a coward trying to save his own skin, he did not want to be put to death. So he denied his Lord whom he had heard and whom he had seen performing these mighty miracles; he denied him in order to save his own life. And yet the moment he is baptized with the Spirit, you see him standing up and addressing that crowd at Jerusalem with fearlessness and boldness, charging them with sin, bringing the message home to them, afraid of no one and of nothing. What a contrast!

Again, we read in Acts 4 that Peter was himself on trial—the very thing he was so afraid of before the baptism with the Spirit. We are told that the authorities 'laid hands on them, and put them in hold unto the next day' (verse 3). Here are Peter and John they are on trial, and then in verse 8 you read: 'Then Peter, filled with the Holy Ghost'—now that was another enduement, that was something special, the Spirit came upon him again with unusual power—'said unto them, Ye rulers of the people, and elders of Israel, If we this day be examined of the good deed done to the impotent man, by what means he is made whole; Be it known unto you all, and to all the people of Israel, that by the name of Jesus Christ of Nazareth, whom ye crucified, whom God raised from the dead, even by him doth this man stand here before you whole' (verses 8-10). Boldness! Fearlessness!

This is what the Holy Spirit does to a man. And you find the same thing later on in that chapter, when again the authorities 'commanded them not to speak at all nor teach in the name of Jesus. But Peter and John answered and said unto them, Whether it be right in the sight of God to hearken unto you more than unto God, judge ye. For we cannot but speak the things which we have seen and heard' (verses 18-20). Now this is obviously one of the great characteristics of the baptism with the Spirit, it gives this boldness and fearlessness.

Let me give you one other example because, my dear friends, if we are not thrilled by this kind of thing, if we do not feel that there is something wrong with us, that we know nothing about this quality, well then, I say, we are almost beyond hope. Read on ... 'Then Peter and the other apostles answered and said' —and they are before the court again—'We ought to obey God rather than men. The God of our fathers raised up Jesus, whom ye slew and hanged on a tree. Him hath God exalted with his right hand to be a Prince and a Saviour, for to give repentance to Israel, and forgiveness of sins. And we are his witnesses of these things; and so is also the Holy Ghost, whom God hath given to them that obey him' (Acts 5:29-32).

Well there it is in the Scripture, and in the long annals of the Christian church is there anything comparable to the way in which the saints of God have been given this same boldness and fearlessness? We know of some of the great notable examples, and for myself these are the things in which I glory, these heroes of the Christian faith defying kings, emperors, princes, the great ones of the world, speaking the truth of God and the truth concerning the Lord Jesus Christ. Think of those early martyrs and confessors, think of those men who were not afraid of a Nero. They would not be subjugated and subdued, they defied him and were ready to be cast to the lions in the arena, praising God that at last they had been accounted worthy to suffer for his name's sake. And down the ages they come, these glorious men, standing up, fighting, defying the 'lion's gory mane' and every principality and power.

But let us not forget this. Among them were large numbers of ordinary common people. As Gray puts it in his 'Elegy in a Country Churchyard', 'Some village Hampden, some unknown Milton'—nobody knows their names. But there have been ordinary men and women who have had to do this very thing and have been threatened with losing their work, turned out of their cottage homes where they and their ancestors had lived for centuries—turned out for one reason only, that they had become Protestants. The annals of the church are full of stories of such people. We do not know their names but we know of them—the common people.

This has been one of the most glorious things in the long history of the Christian church. Boldness! Fearlessness! Not foolhardiness remember, not being ridiculous, but always being ready to give a reason for the hope that is in you, with confidence, with assurance; not allowing yourself to be intimidated by any earthly human power. Your loyalty is to him, and you have been given such a knowledge of him and of his love to you that you are ready to declare it with boldness and fearlessness whatever the consequences may be.

And this is still happening today, even in our own age. We thank God for the martyrs in the Congo, many of whom went through this very experience. It was their boldness, their fearlessness that was such an offence to others. There are endless illustrations which one could give. I have known such people myself, friends who passed through a similar experience with the Communists in China in the 1920s. As long as I live I will never forget hearing Mr and Mrs Porteous of the China Inland Mission telling how with guns facing them and expecting certain death they asked that they might just be allowed to sing before they died. Their request was granted and they sang, 'And I shall see Him face to face, and tell the story, Saved by grace'. God in his mercy used that opportunity to lead to their release and their freedom.

These then are some of the external signs of the baptism in the Spirit and they are clear and obvious to all. I have considered them each in turn so that we all may examine ourselves and ask the question: Is there something about me that makes this impression upon men and women? I am a Christian, as these people were, but is there that quality about me which makes such an impact, leading men and women to consider these matters?

We come now to another division of the work of the Holy Spirit. I confess freely that it is beyond any question the most difficult aspect of the whole subject, and yet we must deal honestly with it because it is in the Scriptures. It is the question of the gifts of the Holy Spirit which result from the baptism with the Spirit. The issue is not an easy one mainly because it is controversial. It has certain inherent difficulties, which often arise because of our ignorance of the spiritual realm, but at this time it is a very important matter for two main reasons. The first is that we need some supernatural authentication of our message; and secondly, it is important because of the danger attending it, because of the enemy, who can counterfeit to such an extent as almost to deceive, according to our Lord and Saviour, 'even the very elect themselves'. This is our Lord's own teaching and warning in Matthew 24:24. He says: 'They shall shew great signs and wonders'—lying signs and wonders, which are so clever and subtle—'that if it were possible, they shall deceive the very elect' themselves.

On the first point, it is becoming clear to everybody—at least it should be—that the Christian church today is failing, and failing lamentably. It is not enough even to be orthodox. You must, of course, be orthodox, otherwise you have not got a message. People are not going to listen to our speculation; they can speculate themselves. People want a word of authority. This has always been so through the ages and we have seen how people recognize this authority. We need authority and we need authentication. It is not enough merely that we state these things and demonstrate them and put them logically. All that is essential but it is not enough. Is it not clear that we are living in an age when we need some special authentication—in other words, we need revival.

Indeed, we are not only confronted by materialism, worldliness, indifference, hardness, and callousness—but we are also hearing more and more, both directly and in the media, about certain manifestations of the powers of evil and the reality of evil spirits. It is not merely sin that is constituting a problem in this country today. There is also a recrudescence of black magic and devil worship and the powers of darkness as well as drug taking and some of the things it leads to. This is why I believe we are in urgent need of some manifestation, some demonstration, of the power of the *Holy Spirit*.

In the New Testament and, indeed, in the whole of the Bible, we are taught that the baptism with the Spirit is attended by certain gifts. Joel in his prophecy, quoted by Peter on the day of Pentecost, foretells this: 'And it shall come to pass in the last days, saith God, that I will pour out my Spirit upon all flesh: and your sons and your daughters shall prophesy, and your young men shall see visions, and your old men shall dream dreams: And on my servants and on my handmaidens I will pour out in those days of my Spirit; and they shall prophesy: And I will shew wonders in heaven above and signs in the earth beneath' (Acts 2:17). Joel, and the other prophets who also spoke of it, indicated that in the age which was to come, and which came with the Lord Jesus Christ and the baptism with the Spirit on the day of Pentecost, there should be some unusual authentication of the message.

And as we see in John 14 our Lord himself prophesied this. In reasoning with the unbelieving, he said: 'If you do not believe me, if you do not believe my words then believe me for the very works' sake.' The Lord's miracles were signs, for that is the term used in the gospel of John with respect to them. The miracles were not only done as acts of kindness. The main reason for them was that they should be 'signs', authentications of who he was.

Our Lord makes this clear when he says: 'Believe me that I am in the Father, and the Father in me: or else believe me for the very works' sake.' And then he goes on: 'I say unto you, He that believeth on me, the works that I do shall he do also; and greater works than these shall he do; because I go unto my Father' (Jn 14:11-12).

Our Lord constantly used this very argument. For instance, when John the Baptist sent two of his disciples to him asking: 'Art thou he that should come, or do we look for another?, Jesus answered and said unto them, Go and shew John again those things which ye do hear and see: The blind receive their sight, and the lame walk, the lepers are cleansed, and the deaf hear, the dead are raised up, and the poor have the gospel preached to them. And blessed is he, whosoever shall not be offended in me' (Mt 11:3-6).

It is clear, then, from all the teaching leading up to the book of Acts that this was to be expected. And as soon as you look at Acts itself, you find the evidence there in great profusion. From the opening chapters we read of 'cloven tongues as of fire', visible signs, miracles of various descriptions, prophetic utterances and so on. Such manifestations of the Spirit run right through the book of Acts. But what is interesting is that they are not confined to Acts. You find exactly the same thing being taught in the various epistles. Take, for instance, the famous passage in 1 Corinthians from chapter 12 right to the end of chapter 14. These chapters deal exclusively with this great matter, showing that in the church at Corinth, as in all the other churches, this kind of thing was taking place and so the apostle has to deal with the situation.

And, indeed, in 2 Corinthians 12:12 where the whole question of his being an apostle has been raised by certain enemies and detractors, Paul writes: 'Truly the signs of an apostle were wrought among you in all patience, in signs and wonders, and mighty deeds.' The apostle's ministry was authenticated in that way.

And then in Galatians 3:2 he says: 'This only would I learn of you, Received ye the Spirit by the works of the law, or by the hearing of faith?' And then in verse 5: 'He therefore that ministereth to you the Spirit, and worketh miracles among you, doeth he it by the works of the law, or by the hearing of faith?' Now the apostle says that the Spirit came upon those who had believed by faith. It is to believers that the Spirit is given in this way in baptism. The result was that God ministered the Spirit to them and miracles were being worked among them, and the apostle uses the same argument in that respect.

Let me give you a final illustration of what I am trying to show from Hebrews 2:3-4. The author talks about the gospel 'which at the first began to be spoken by the Lord, and was confirmed unto us by them that heard him; God also bearing them witness, both with signs and wonders, and with divers miracles, and gifts of the Holy Ghost, according to his own will?'

I am simply trying to establish the point that it is perfectly clear that in New Testament times, the gospel was authenticated in this way by signs, wonders and miracles of various characters and descriptions. And you cannot begin to understand the New Testament, the epistles as well as the book of Acts without holding that fact in your mind and seeing that that is clearly the case.

Now I believe I am right in saying that everyone who is a Christian in any sense at all is prepared to believe and to accept that these things happened, but it is here that the vital question arises—do we accept it as being only true of the early church? Was it only meant to be true of the early church? This is the question to which we must now address ourselves. There are many people who teach that. They say, 'Of course I accept the whole of that evidence'—though they may try to water even that down. I have known people who have tried to explain away things that are clearly miraculous —the cloven tongues of fire, and the speaking in other languages on the day of Pentecost. I have heard men using the greatest ingenuity to try to explain it all away, claiming some knowledge which they have just received about some odd dialects and so on.

But I am not wasting my time with that kind of argument. I am dealing with people who say, 'Of course I accept everything that I find in the New Testament. I am sure it is historical and that these things actually happened. But that really does not apply to us now, it was only meant for that time'. They may also suggest that all this was really meant as a sign to convince the unbelieving Jews. Take our Lord's answer to John the Baptist. John was a typical Jew and our Lord says to him, 'Look the signs that were prophesied are taking place, there is your answer.' And this leads those people to say that all these signs and miracles in the New Testament period were solely designed to appeal to the Jews and to convince them.

For example, one writer actually says that after our Lord's own failure in his teaching—he came to found the kingdom and hoped he would persuade the Jews to follow him, but he did not succeed and they put him to death—the church was a kind of afterthought and God then made his last effort on the day of Pentecost in the sending of this miraculous power among the apostles. It was the final appeal to the Jews.

As a result of accepting this interpretation, when they come to the disciples in Acts 19, whom Paul came across at Ephesus and to whom he put the question: 'Did you receive the Holy Ghost when you believed?', they have to say, 'Of course, these again were obviously Jews', although there is not a word to support this assumption. In fact, most authorities are agreed that these people almost certainly had some connection with Alexandria in Egypt. Certainly that was the case, as we know, with regard to Apollos. However, they do not hesitate to state quite dogmatically that these people were Jews, and that because of that they were given the particular sign of tongues in order to convince them.

Another way in which the argument is put is to agree that those extraordinary signs were given then, but that was because it was the beginning of the Christian church, and God, as it were, did the unusual to get the church going. They say that the same kind of thing happened in the Old Testament at the beginning of the great line of prophets, in Elijah and Elisha, where you read that they performed certain miracles. These expositors maintain that you always tend to get this sort of thing at the beginning of a work, but that of course you do not expect it to go on. It is like a father setting up his son by giving him a farm or a business. He puts a sum of money in the bank for him and then says, 'get on with it'. He does not go on giving him these gifts, after setting him up, this is something unusual and exceptional at the beginning of a work. So they say that these things did happen, but it was only meant to mark the beginning of the dispensation.

Another argument is that these things happened, these signs were given and so unusual powers and manifestations did occur, but only until the New Testament canon was completed. When the church began Christians did not have the New Testament epistles. But we have them, we have the full truth in the words of Scripture, which we can read, study, expound, and understand. The early church could not do that, so God gave revelations to apostles and to prophets and to certain other people at certain times; they were dependent upon this direct message and teaching. But the moment the church was given the Scriptures, all that was no longer necessary. We have got the truth so you do not need anything miraculous or supernatural.

These expositors are particularly fond of arguing that point in terms of 1 Corinthians 13. One writer actually puts it like this: 'After the Scriptures were completed these supernatural signs ceased.' He makes a dogmatic pronouncement, and says that they ceased because they were no longer necessary once we had the Scriptures. The argument which they try to put forward is as follows: Paul says in 1 Corinthians 13:8-10: 'Charity never faileth: but whether there be prophecies, they shall fail; whether there be tongues, they shall cease; whether there be knowledge, it shall vanish away. For we know in part, and we prophesy in part. But when that which is perfect is come, then that which is in part shall be done away.'

They argue that 'that which is perfect' is the giving of the New Testament Scriptures and once they were given 'that which is in part shall be done away.' 1 Corinthians 13:11 continues: 'When I was a child, I spake as a child, I understood as a child, I thought as a child: but when I became a man, I put away childish things'—such as prophecy and speaking in tongues and miracles and things like that—'I put away childish things.' 'For now', Paul goes on, 'we see through a glass, darkly; but then face to face.' That is, they maintain, when you get the Scriptures: 'Now I know in part; but then shall I know even as also I am known.'

For the proponents of this view all this means that until the Scriptures came knowledge was very partial and the apostle is quite clearly saying here that all these partial, supernatural manifestations belong to the realm of childish things which will vanish away when the perfection and the fullness comes, and that did come when the New Testament canon was completed. Added to this they produce a subsidiary argument and go so far as to say that even in the New Testament itself you have clear evidence that these things were already passing away. They cite the fact that Paul could not heal Timothy and has to tell him to take a little wine for his stomach's sake, that Trophimus was left sick and ill at Miletum, that Gaius was not healed, and that Epaphroditus was desperately ill, 'nigh unto death', but that the Lord had had mercy upon him and that he had got well again. They say therefore that even in the New Testament itself you see these things passing—starting on the day of Pentecost in great fullness, but gradually disappearing as you go on in the New Testament.

And so they come to a final conclusion, which they state with the utmost confidence and dogmatism, that after the coming of the New Testament canon all these gifts were entirely withdrawn.

There, then, is an outline of the argument that is being put forward at the present time, and which has been put forward very largely during this present century. Let me begin to answer it by giving you just one thought at this point. It is this: the Scriptures never anywhere say that these things were only temporary—never! There is no such statement anywhere. 'Ah but', says somebody, 'what about that passage from 1 Corinthians 13?' Well, I would have thought that that chapter is sufficient answer in and of itself to this particular criticism. You see what we are asked to believe by that kind of exposition? We are told that the coming of the New Testament Scriptures puts us into a place of perfection; whereas if you look at verse 12 it actually says: 'For now we see'—that is the apostle and others. The apostle is included with all other Christian believers before the New Testament canon, much of which was written by Paul himself, had been completed. We read: 'Now we see through a glass, darkly; but then'—when the Scriptures have come and are complete —'face to face: Now I know in part; but then'—which they say means the completion of the Scriptures—'shall I know even as also I am known.'

You see what that involves? It means that you and I, who have the Scriptures open before us, know much more than the apostle Paul of God's truth. That is what it means and nothing less, if that argument is correct. It means that we are altogether superior to the early church and even to the apostles themselves, including the apostle Paul! It means that we are now in a position in which we know 'face to face' that 'we know, even as also we are known' by God because we have the Scriptures. It is surely unnecessary to say more.

What the apostle is, of course, dealing with in 1 Corinthians 13 is the contrast between the highest and the best that the Christian can ever know in this world and in this life and what he will know in the glory everlasting. The 'now' and the 'then' are not the time before and after the Scriptures were given, because that, as I have said, puts us in a position entirely superior to the apostles and prophets who are the foundation of the Christian church and on whose very work we have to rely. It is inconsistent, and contradictory—indeed, there is only one word to describe such a view, it is nonsense. The 'then' is the glory everlasting. It is only then that I shall know, even as also I am known; for then we shall see him as he is. It will be direct and 'face to face'. No longer, as Paul puts it again in 2 Corinthians 3:18—as an image or a reflection, but direct, absolute, full and perfect knowledge.

So you see the difficulties men land themselves in when they dislike something and cannot fully understand it and try to explain it away. All things must be judged in the light of the Scriptures, and we must not twist them to suit our theory or argument. Let me finish with this general statement—there is nothing in the Scripture itself which says that these things are to end, and further, every attempt to make the Scriptures say that leads to the same dismal, impossible conclusions that we have already seen in the case of 1 Corinthians 13.

My friends, this is to me one of the most urgent matters at this hour. With the church as she is and the world as it is, the greatest need today is the power of God through his Spirit in the church that we may testify not only to the power of the Spirit, but to the glory and the praise of the one and only Saviour, Jesus Christ our Lord, Son of God, Son of Man.

Chapter 2

'As the Spirit Wills'

We have been considering those words of John the Baptist when he proclaimed the One who would baptize with the Holy Spirit. In these verses John the Baptist indicates what is to be the outstanding characteristic of the age of the Lord Jesus Christ and of his ministry. It is, therefore, something which we should be clear about in our minds as it obviously controls the whole of the New Testament teaching. And so we have been looking at it and examining the teaching that we have here concerning it which is abundantly confirmed in the subsequent history of the Christian church.

Now this is of importance to us for so many reasons. Primarily I would suggest that we must be concerned about this, because we as Christian people are to be concerned about the state of the world in which we live and the state of the church. The church seems so weak and ineffective in this modern world, and so filled with troubles that the problem of what we can do about the situation should be uppermost in the minds of all Christian people.

We read the New Testament and we see the great power that was given to the early apostles and disciples. Their world was very similar to ours: we recognize the sin and aberrations, the perversions and the foulness, the moral degradation that we read of in parts of the New Testament. And yet we find that just a handful of simple, unlettered, ignorant men and women were able, not only to make an impact upon that world, but to influence it and to influence it profoundly. The explanation is, of course, that they were baptized with the Holy Spirit. What John the Baptist prophesied, what our Lord himself prophesied, literally came to pass. And the only explanation of the New Testament church and the astounding things that she was enabled to do in later centuries is this power that was given by the baptism with the Holy Spirit. As we have seen it is essentially something that is given to enable us to witness: 'Ye shall receive power . . .', says our Lord, 'and ye shall be witnesses unto me' (Acts 1:8). Its primary object is to make us witnesses, people who testify to God and his redeeming grace in and through our blessed Lord and Saviour. Our Lord said of the Spirit, 'He shall glorify me.' Not himself. And the business of the witness is to bear witness to the Lord Jesus Christ as the Son of God and the only Saviour. And now we have come to this great question of the gifts, the spiritual gifts which are given by the Spirit to men and women in order to enable them to become witnesses.

This is not only a great subject, it has, alas, also become a controversial one, and that is why we must examine it very carefully. There is teaching about this in Scripture and it is our business to know the Scriptures and to expound them. We must not side-step anything taught in the Scriptures as being too difficult or controversial. We must examine it in the Spirit, not to prove our case or our point, but to arrive at a knowledge of the truth that we may glorify our Lord and, through him, glorify God, the Eternal Father.

At the present time there is a new interest in this matter in the United States and in this country, and in many other parts of the world, and it behoves us as Christian people to clarify our minds, to seek a true understanding in the light of the scriptural teaching. That is what we are now trying to do, and we are endeavouring to do it thoroughly. I do not believe in short cuts or glib answers; they are never satisfactory. They always leave something out of account. So let us go on quietly, and let us pray God to give us the spirit of understanding that we may lay hold on these things which clearly are difficult. That is why they had to be dealt with in epistles in the first century, and it is still as essential today that these matters should be understood at the present time.

We saw earlier that some people believe that the gifts were withdrawn when the New Testament canon was complete. Some of them go so far as to say that church history shows clearly that these gifts were withdrawn; and some say quite dogmatically that they have never occurred since—that there has literally been no miracle since these New Testament times. And there are those who actually go further—I have read a number of their booklets recently—and say beyond any question that what are claimed to be manifestations of the gifts of the Spirit are nothing but the manifestations of 'devilish power'. And they say that in cold print! Christian people actually write and publish these things.

But they base it on this argument and in this they are quite logical. They say all this was only meant for the time of the New Testament church and finished then, therefore anything that may appear to be a supernatural gift since then must of necessity be 'of the devil', a counterfeit, something to be avoided as the very plague itself, and indeed, something which is extremely dangerous.

We have already dealt with the wrong interpretation of 1 Corinthians 13 but we must go on with this argument so that this most important point may be made very clear. If these people are right and these gifts were only meant for that particular time and that can be proved, then there is no need to say any more. However, I want to suggest to you that that is not the case. Take the argument that the gifts were meant only for the Jews. It seems to me that the book of Acts is sufficient in and of itself to give us an answer—an answer that is also supported in the epistles.

Let me explain .... The book of Acts shows very clearly that many miracles were performed among the Gentiles as 'signs'. Indeed, reading Acts I cannot see how anybody can come to any conclusion but this—that generally speaking when he was dealing with Jews the apostle Paul 'reasoned with them from the scriptures'. For instance, there is a perfect illustration of that in Acts 17, where we are told how Paul, when he arrived at Thessalonica, went into the synagogue of the Jews. Then we read: 'And Paul, as his manner was, went in unto them, and three sabbath days reasoned with them out of the scriptures, opening and alleging, that Christ must needs have suffered, and risen again from the dead; and that this Jesus, whom I preach unto you, is Christ' (verses 2-3).

That is obviously a very reasonable procedure. Here were Jews who boasted in their Old Testament Scriptures, so the Apostle simply shows them 'out of the scriptures' that Jesus is the Christ, and that it was prophesied that the Christ was not going to be a great military conqueror, but that he was going to be one who was going to suffer, be 'led as a lamb to the slaughter'. The Apostle almost invariably approached Jews in this way. It was what our Lord himself had done after his resurrection with the disciples themselves. They had been stumbled by the cross, so our Lord took them through the prophets and Moses and the Psalms, and demonstrated to them from the Scriptures.

When dealing with a Jew who has got the Scriptures and who knows them, that is obviously the procedure to adopt, and that is what the apostles did. But when you are dealing with Gentiles you cannot do that, because they do not know the Scriptures, and do not have the same background. You can only begin to do that with them after a while, after you have given them instruction concerning the Old Testament Scriptures. So what we find is that when the apostles work amongst the Gentiles they generally work large numbers of miracles.

There are many examples of this such as Acts 14 when Paul is in Lystra and Acts 16 where Paul at Philippi ministered to the girl with a spirit of divination. Then in Acts 19 there is a most interesting phrase which is used about Paul at Ephesus: 'God wrought special miracles by the hands of Paul' (verse 11). Now that was in a Gentile community, so this idea that such signs were only for the Jews seems to me to be something that simply cannot be substantiated at all from the book of Acts—indeed it is almost the exact opposite as one would expect. It seems that this great profusion of miracles was wrought among Gentiles, who could not be reasoned with out of the Scriptures because they did not know them. Without the authority of Scripture they needed this other authentication. And indeed we read further about Paul: 'So that from his body were brought unto the sick handkerchiefs or aprons, and the diseases departed from them, and the evil spirits went out of them' (verse 12), and it led to that trouble which ended in a riot in Ephesus.

Then take another statement which is based upon the fact that these things are not mentioned in the pastoral epistles or in what are regarded as the later epistles of the apostle Paul. Some people deduce that they are not mentioned because they had already disappeared. Now this, it seems to me, is a most dangerous argument. It is what is called the argument from silence. Because the apostle, in the pastoral epistles and in epistles like that to the Colossians, does not deal with the question of the gifts as he does in 1 Corinthians, it is presumed that these gifts had already been withdrawn even before the end of the New Testament canon.

Let me give you just one illustration of what I mean. I read an article on this very subject recently which shows how men with a bias and a prejudice are so governed by it that they read things into the Scriptures which are not there and so draw their false deductions. Let me quote from that article: 'St. Paul indeed hardly mentions the gift'—the writer is dealing with 'tongues' in particular—'except to try to regulate the behaviour of those who possess it and to check its misuse.' Then he goes on: 'It was no doubt this that led him to relegate the gift to the bottom of the list of charismata and to urge his readers to try and get it in perspective.' All right. But then he says, 'To him it was permissible rather than desirable.' 'Permissible rather than desirable!' But the Apostle says himself quite clearly in 1 Corinthians 14, 'I would that ye all spake in tongues.' Now that is not merely permissible; that is desirable! The writer goes on to say this: 'Is there any significance in the fact that the Corinthian Church, where alone it appears that the practice prevailed . . . .' You see, he is assuming, because it is not mentioned concerning the other churches, that it did not occur there. Now that is nothing but argument from silence. It is deduction. But let us go on. 'Is there any significance in the fact that the Corinthian Church, where alone it appears that the practice prevailed, was morally and spiritually the least mature in the early Christian communities?' There is no evidence at all for saying that. We do not know that the Corinthian church was the 'least mature'. There is evidence to suggest that the churches at Thessalonica and in Galatia were equally immature.

This is all pure conjecture; it is reading into the Scriptures in order to substantiate your particular prejudice. The writer proceeds, 'I know St. Paul said, "Thank God I am more gifted in ecstatic utterance than any of you'"—but Paul did not actually say that, he said 'speak in tongues' (1 Cor 14:18). Some would say that it is not 'ecstatic utterance'. I happen to agree with the interpretation, which says that it is ecstatic utterance but it should not be used as if it were a translation. The writer is now putting in 'ecstatic utterance' in the place of 'other tongues'—he goes on: '. . . but was the inference not simply that he knew what he was talking about when he urged his readers not to set great store on this gift?' I suggest that it means much more than that and I hope to deal with that later on.

'I do not know', this man continues quite honestly, 'I would not like to dogmatize'—and yet that is what he has been doing, for this is what we all tend to do—'but at least I have never had these questions answered in a really satisfactory way.'

It seems to me that the answer is in the Scriptures themselves—and that if you take them as they are, you find that you are not entitled to make these statements. 'I would that ye all spake in tongues.' Not permissible only but even desirable! Again, 'Forbid not', Paul says, 'to speak in tongues.' I suggest, then, that when he says: 'I thank God, I speak in tongues more than you all', he is not merely claiming that he knows more about this than they do in a sense of having knowledge about it, he is in fact claiming something experiential and experimental.

So we must beware that we do not try to avoid these things or get rid of them merely by making assumptions. It is always most dangerous to deduce something merely from silence. The epistles were all written for a specific purpose. In Corinth there was a great deal of confusion because of the gifts and the Apostle deals with it at great length. In other churches the gifts were present with equal profusion as suggested by 1 Corinthians 1:47 and 1 Thessalonians 5:19-21, but because they were not being misunderstood and because people were not getting too excited about them there was no need to deal with the question. So the explanation of why these things are not mentioned in other places is probably that they did not constitute problems.

We must get one thing clear in our minds. These epistles were not written as textbooks on theology or on the doctrine of the church. They were all written to meet some particular situation. Take for instance the epistle to the Colossians. Now there the big problem was the philosophical speculations that were coming in. So the Apostle deals with that. He does not set down on paper a complete treatise on the whole of church doctrine. The apostles were busy men, travelling and evangelizing and they wrote their letters to deal with particular problems as they arose; and if you bear that in mind, you will have a new and a fresh understanding of all these epistles. In Galatia the great question was that of circumcision, but it was not the only problem. As I have already quoted from Galatians 3:2,5, the apostle refers, just in passing, to the fact that miracles were being worked there. But whereas there were problems in the Corinthian church over gifts, Paul does not have to deal with any problems arising from the miracles, as far as the churches in Galatia were concerned.

So the principle is, be careful lest you base your argument solely on this argument from silence. It is a notorious trap. It has accounted for many heresies throughout the centuries. We must take the Scriptures as a whole, and, as I have been trying to remind you, the background to the whole of the New Testament writings is the history of the Acts of the Apostles. You must not found your doctrine on the epistles only. The epistles are to be read in the light of the history that is given us so plainly in Acts.

Let us, then, go on to another argument. We read that Timothy is exhorted to 'take a little wine for his stomach's sake' instead of being miraculously healed, that 'Trophimus was left sick at Miletum', that 'Epaphroditus had been desperately ill so that they had even despaired of his life and feared that he was on the verge of death'. The argument based on these facts is that miracles had obviously been withdrawn, or these men would have been healed at once; there would have been no need to give medical advice to Timothy and this kind of prescription would have been quite unnecessary.

Now that is the assumption. But the New Testament nowhere tells us that sickness must always be healed, and always be healed miraculously. Some people who believe that these gifts are permanent and who claim miraculous healing today go so far as to say a Christian should never be ill and that he should always be healed miraculously. The other extreme is to assume that the fact that these men were not immediately healed is proof that the miraculous was immediately withdrawn.

Both these views are guilty of the same error, which is to assume that in the New Testament any Christian taken ill should be healed miraculously. But the New Testament never teaches that. A miracle is an exceptional thing, which only happens sometimes.

The real answer to this whole question is the apostle's statement in 2 Corinthians 12 where he deals with his own thorn in the flesh. The apostle himself tended to fall into this error. He was taken ill and could not do his work, so prayed that God should take it away. But it was not taken away. He prayed three times and was most urgent about it. Here is a man who had performed tremendous miracles and had seen astounding things and yet when he is ill himself he has to endure his illness. But he was taught the reason for this. He was taught that there is something more important than physical healing, and that is one's knowledge of God. This great lesson, 'My grace is sufficient for thee.' He had not known that before as he should have done.

The Bible teaches that illness is sometimes permitted for the good of our soul. God permits things to happen to us for our good. Now that does not mean that every sickness is always permitted by God for our good; there are secondary causes—the world is a world of sin and disease has come in. All I am saying is that sometimes this is true. That is all the Apostle says. In his particular case the thorn in the flesh was not removed in order that he might learn that 'When I am weak, then am I strong'.

So the principle is established that you must not argue that because some men in the New Testament were not miraculously healed, that the miraculous power had therefore been withdrawn. The miracles, including the power of healing, were always something occasional, determined by the Spirit. It did not happen automatically that every Christian was immediately healed. Some men were healed, some were not. God has a purpose in all these matters. All these gifts, as I shall be emphasizing, are under the sovereignty of the Spirit. He decides when and how and where. We must never think of it as automatic, that you just pull a lever and there it is, it has all happened. That is entirely foreign to the New Testament. A power was given, a commission was given on particular occasions, and then the miracles happened.

But let me take you on to another argument which to me is a very important one. It seems that this idea that these things belong only to the New Testament period and have nothing to do with us is really guilty of the error known as 'higher criticism'. This is the error which sits in judgement on the Scriptures and says, 'Of course, yes, that was only temporary, that does not apply to us.' You decide what is acceptable and what is not. You pick and choose. This argument is exactly the same.

In other words that whole section of 1 Corinthians, we are told, has nothing to do with us because that was a temporary position. But in that case, was not the whole of the New Testament church a temporary position? It was a church that was filled with the Spirit; 'miracles and signs and wonders' were taking place. We have considered the quotation which demonstrates that fact in Hebrews 2:4 and again I would remind you of the statement in Galatians 3:5. The New Testament church was a pneumatic church that was filled with the Spirit and these things were happening. The whole of the New Testament church was in that condition. So then to be logical, these friends ought to say that the whole of the New Testament does not apply to us at all, that it has nothing to say to us, because the position is now quite different since we have got the Scriptures. But the argument turns back upon itself. The Scriptures which we have are those which deal with the New Testament church, and therefore if they have any relevance to us we must be essentially in the same position as the New Testament church itself.

We must beware, then, of a teaching which judges the Scriptures and says, 'This applies to us, that does not'.

Having thus dealt with the arguments in a purely scriptural manner, let me adduce history. Take this idea that all miraculous gifts and manifestations ended with the apostolic age. Now here, surely, is something that we have no right to state dogmatically, because there is clear historical evidence that many of these gifts persisted for several centuries. There are authentic records in the lives and writings of some of the great Fathers of the church—Tertullian and others—which leave us in no doubt that these things did persist.

But more than that—and this to me is very important—there is great evidence of these things even at the time of the Protestant Reformation. Have you ever read the life story of that great man and scholar John Welsh, the son-in-law of John Knox? There are amazing things which appear to be well authenticated in connection with him. There is a tradition, which has been repeated by the most sober-minded historians, that on one occasion, when he was living in exile in the south of France, John Welsh actually raised someone from the dead. Now I do not know, I just put the evidence before you. All I am trying to say is that I would not dare to assert that these things ended with the apostolic age and that there has never been a miracle since. Indeed, I do not believe it! There is evidence, from many of those Protestant Reformers and Fathers, that some of them had a genuine true gift of prophecy—I mean by that foretelling events. And you find among the Scottish Covenanters people like Alexander Peden and others who gave accurate, literal prophecies of things that subsequently took place.

Let me put it at its very lowest to you. I feel that what needs to be said to this generation in which we are living is this: 'There are more things in heaven and earth, Horatio, than are dreamt of in your philosophy.' Our danger is to quench the Spirit and to put a limit upon the power of God, the Holy Spirit. Have you ever read the life of Pastor Hsi of China? Can you deny the miraculous in that story?—the manifestation of some of these same gifts that were so clear in the history of the early church? Throughout the centuries books have been written on this great theme. Horace Bushnell, a preacher and theologian in America in the last century, dealt with this very thoroughly and marshalled a great deal of evidence. There is further evidence in the Woodrow collection of biographies mainly connected with Scottish worthies and in *Men of the Covenant* by Alexander Smellie.

I commend you to read these books and there you will find this gift of prophecy that was given to men to see the future, the power of speech that was given to them, and the occasional miracle. Anyone who is prepared to say that all this ended with the apostolic age, and that there has never been a miracle since the apostles, is making a most daring statement. Not only is there nothing in the Scripture to say that all these miraculous gifts had to end with the apostolic age; the subsequent history of the church, it seems to me, gives the lie direct to this very contention.

I say once more, therefore, that to hold such a view is simply to quench the Spirit. And surely, we must deduce from the Scriptures that if you say that the Holy Spirit was given to the early church to start it off, then these things are necessary, indeed essential, at all times when the church is down in the depths and the world is loud and strong and powerful. Surely that is just the time when you would expect a manifestation of some such power. If the apostles were incapable of being true witnesses without unusual power, who are we to claim that we can be witnesses without such power?

There then is the main argument. There are also certain trivial arguments which I mention merely in order to dismiss them. Many people at the present time say: 'You mustn't touch this subject, because it is only producing strife and division among Christian people.' This I find really very pathetic; that is the charge that has always been brought against Evangelicals, it was the charge that was brought indeed against Martin Luther, indeed it was the charge that was brought against the Puritans—'Why wouldn't they keep the ranks, why must they be separatist and claiming....?' It is the argument that was brought against the Methodists, that has indeed been brought against Evangelicals whenever they have been called to witness for God in a special manner. Down through the ages they have been accused of causing division and strife and separation. Be careful, though, for if you press that argument we shall all be back in Rome, for it is ultimately the Roman argument against the whole of Protestantism—these separated 'Brethren' who made the mistake of going out.

But then there is another minor argument. It is said that people who are concerned about these things manifest a feeling of superiority, despise others and look down upon those who do not have these gifts or who have not received the baptism with the Holy Spirit. Again the answer is exactly the same; that has always been the argument of a traditional dead church against anybody who receives new life from the Spirit. It is invariable. It was, indeed, the argument of the Pharisees against our Lord.

So far we have been dealing with the attempt to dismiss the whole of this question on the basis that it only belonged to the New Testament period and therefore has nothing to do with us. Now I want to deal with the exact opposite position. It is interesting to notice how you always get the extremes.

The second position is that of those who assert that the full and miraculous gifts of the Holy Spirit ought always to abide in the church, and that it is only from want of faith that we do not possess them now. Some of them go further and say that we ought to 'claim' these gifts. These people maintain that these gifts were meant not only for the New Testament church but for the church at all times and the church today, they say, would be thrilling with all these gifts were it not for our lack of faith. They ought always to be present even as they were in the early church.

I want to suggest to you that this position is also unscriptural and once again finds no warrant in the Scripture itself. The teaching of the Scripture is that these things are to be considered in terms of the lordship of the Spirit. It is he who decides. 'He giveth to every man severally as he wills.' It is he who chooses. That was the whole trouble in Corinth, where they were all claiming 'all the gifts', as it were. And the answer to them is that he gives one this and the other one that. It is all entirely within his control. He decides when, how, to whom, and where.

Let me put this argument in the way which has always been most helpful to me. This is exactly the same as the question of revival. A revival by definition is not something permanent. It is something that comes, and goes, and comes, and goes. The history of the church has been the history of revivals. There have always been people who have taught that you can get a revival whenever you like. All you have to do is to pray, or to do certain things and to claim it, and you get revival. But the simple answer is, You cannot! I have known some of the best, most honest and saintly men who have fallen into that error; *you* cannot decide when revival comes. It always comes in the sovereignty of the Spirit. It often comes when you least expect it. It can come in the most unlikely quarter, and the man used can be the most unlikely sort of man.

The same principle applies to the gifts of the Spirit. We must not legislate on one side or the other. We must not say 'only' for New Testament times nor must we say 'always'. The answer is, 'as he wills', as the Spirit wills. It is always right to seek the fullness of the Spirit—we are exhorted to do so. But the gifts of the Spirit are to be left in the hands of the Holy Spirit himself.

Finally, I should like to draw your attention to three further points. In the light of the teaching of the sovereignty of the Spirit we are entitled to deduce, firstly, that gifts may be withheld as well as given in the sovereignty of the Spirit. He can withhold them as well as give them. We must never forget that for it is an essential part of this whole notion of sovereignty.

Secondly, we must never use the word 'claim'. It is incompatible with sovereignty. People say, 'Claim this gift;

claim healing.' You cannot claim healing. The Apostle himself claimed healing three times and did not get it. Never claim; never even use the word. We are to submit ourselves —it is the Spirit who gives. The claiming of gifts, or claiming even the baptism of the Spirit, is something that is clearly incompatible with the whole of the New Testament emphasis. No, no, he is Lord, he controls and he gives. You can supplicate but you must never claim. Never!

Then, thirdly, a variation is clearly seen in the New Testament, as I have already shown you. Things do not always happen even when the apostles expect them to happen. And the variation again is to be explained solely in terms of the sovereignty of the Spirit. This is supported and substantiated by the history of revivals, and, indeed, beyond that. There is very clear evidence, it seems to me, that generally at the beginning of any new work, something unusual does happen. I have mentioned the period of the Reformation, and the beginning of missionary work in China and so on .... The unusual happened and this is again in entire accord with the doctrine of the sovereignty of the Spirit.

But I also want to say this—and here is something that is very frequently forgotten. We have noted the argument of people who say: 'These things stopped at the time of the apostles. You do not get these things going on in the history of the church, therefore they were not meant to go on.' But there is another very important side to that question. It is historically true that as you read the history of the church in the first five or six centuries you find less and less evidence of these supernatural powers. And inevitably the question arises, 'Why was that?' These people assume, 'Obviously, they were withdrawn; they were not meant to continue.' I suggest to you that there is a much better answer, which lies in what happened to the life of the church herself. In the second century the church, as she was spreading increasingly amongst the Greeks, wanted to present her gospel in a learned, philosophical manner. There were men called Apologists, who tried to show that the gospel was not incompatible with Greek philosophy and with Roman law. They did so very largely because of persecutions and misunderstandings, and although they set out with good motives they were actually quenching the Spirit by turning the gospel into a 'reasonable' philosophy.

To make matters worse, the Emperor Constantine in his 'wisdom' decided to become a Christian and to bring the Roman Empire into Christianity. The church now became an institution, where everything was controlled; a kind of higher monarchical system came in, and metropolitans were introduced. In other words, the church by the end of the third or fourth century was a church that one simply cannot identify with the church of the New Testament. Not because God had withdrawn the gifts but because man had taken charge of the church and the Spirit was not given opportunity but was being quenched. The institutional church in time gave rise to the Roman Catholic Church of the Middle Ages.

And what is so interesting is that the bogus church always produces bogus miracles. They deny New Testament gifts but they produce bogus miracles, generally in terms of the virgin Mary. How easily we can go astray. We say, 'If you read your history, you will find that these supernatural gifts did not happen for a few centuries.' But we do not ask, 'Why did they not happen?' Or if we do, we give the wrong answer. It is not that God withdrew, it is that the church in her 'wisdom' and cleverness became institutionalized, quenched the Spirit, and made the manifestations of the power of the Spirit well-nigh impossible.

So my final conclusion is this: in the sovereignty of the Spirit these things are always possible. Always possible! I am saying no more. That does not mean that every claim is right. All I am arguing is that on the basis of the teaching of the Scriptures plus the history of the church, these things are always possible. They are especially needed in times of declension, and they have generally characterized some new work on the part of the Holy Spirit of God.

You must not say, 'They never can happen, they were only for the New Testament church. . . .' Nor must you say they should always be present in their fullness. Both views are wrong. But they are always possible! And therefore when we are confronted by something that claims to be a revival or a new giving of such gifts, we must not reject it out of hand, but we must prove it, we must test it. And thank God we are not only exhorted by the Scriptures to do so because of the terrible danger of counterfeits, we are even told and instructed as to how we are to conduct the test.

Chapter 3

Test the Spirits

At this point in our consideration of the gifts of the Holy Spirit, I want briefly to support the conclusion at which we have arrived by adducing again the evidence of history, the history of the church, and particularly the history of revivals.

A revival of religion is nothing but a great outpouring of the Spirit of God upon the church, a kind of repetition of what happened on the day of Pentecost. A revival, in other words, is a number of people being baptized with the Holy Spirit at the same time. You hear or read of Christian people who were doing their best to live the Christian life. They had the assurance of their salvation, which they deduced by examining themselves in the light of the Scriptures, and, indeed, they possessed a spirit within themselves that enabled them in a measure to say 'Abba, Father'. But suddenly the Spirit of God descends upon them. Suddenly they are lifted up to a new height and a new level. They are given an assurance such as they never had before, and they see things with great understanding and luminosity.

Now that is what we mean by revival and, as I have reminded you, there are always certain phenomena attendant upon such visitations of the Spirit of God. We need not go into the details, but there is this new power, and sometimes a kind of prophetic gift is given. Yet it is interesting to observe that in the great revivals in the church throughout the centuries, there has not been very much by way of manifestation of some of these particular gifts, such as the gift of tongues or evidence of miracles.

That is to me a most important point. I am not saying that such gifts are altogether absent, but that they are uncommon and unusual. I am thinking, for instance, of the revivals of 1859 in Northern Ireland, 1857 in America and in other countries, and of the great Evangelical Revival of the eighteenth century in Britain. They were undoubtedly revivals, but there was very little by way of miracles, practically nothing by way of gift of tongues and prophetic utterances. Now these are simply facts that I am putting before you—facts that are well attested and well established.

Why do I make this point? Well, I do so for this reason, and to me it is a very vital one. It is, indeed, my main purpose in this whole series of sermons. It seems to me that the teaching of the Scripture itself, plus the evidence of the history of the church, establishes the fact that the baptism with the Spirit is not always accompanied by particular gifts.

Those who are interested in the contemporary discussion will realize the importance of that statement. There are people today, as there have been now for a number of years, who say that the baptism with the Spirit is always accompanied by certain particular gifts. It seems to me that the answer of the Scripture is that that is not the case, that you may have a baptism with the Spirit, and a mighty baptism with the Spirit at that, with none of the gifts of tongues, miracles, or various other gifts. No one can dispute the baptism with the Spirit in the case of men like the brothers Wesley, and Whitefield and many others, but none of these things happened in connection with them.

Now that, I feel, establishes this all-important principle,

that you must draw a distinction between the baptism with the Spirit itself and its occasional or possible concomitants. We must keep these things distinct in our minds. There is great confusion at this point. In my earlier sermons [*Joy Unspeakable,*—ed.], I have already drawn attention to the way in which people get confused between the baptism with the Spirit and sanctification, which leads to great trouble. This confusion between the baptism and the gifts of the Spirit leads to equally great trouble. I am very anxious to bring out this point with great clarity that the baptism of the Spirit itself may be present in great power and yet none of these gifts may be manifest as such.

That is, of course, because of the sovereignty of the Spirit. He chooses to give them at times, and equally not to give them at others. And we must submit to that and be ready for that. We must not say that gifts cannot happen, nor must we say that they should always happen. The scriptural position, substantiated by the history of the church, is that they may or may not happen, and therefore we must not lay down these dogmatic positions on the one side or on the other. So, then, the main conclusion stands—that this question of gifts is entirely within the sovereignty of the Spirit and that because of that we should always be open, in mind and in heart, to anything that the Spirit of God may choose to do in his sovereignty.

It is very important that we should be concerned about the truth about the baptism in the Spirit for one main reason and that is the state both of the world in which we are living, and that of the church. If you, my friend, as a Christian are not concerned at this moment more than anything else with the need of the power of the Holy Spirit in the Christian church, I am afraid I do not understand your Christianity. Never was there such need of the proclamation of the truth with authority and power, and nothing but a baptism with the Spirit will enable the church to do this. It is God's way at all times. Never was there greater need of our being clear on the doctrine of the baptism with the Spirit, or revival of religion if you like to take it collectively, than at this present time.

As this question of gifts is involved with it, we must examine it, because there are many people who reject the doctrine of the baptism, because they reject the gifts. Again, there are others who, rejecting the false 'coalition', as it were, of sanctification and the baptism, reject the baptism because they feel the claims to entire sanctification cannot be verified or substantiated. What should be of concern to us is the power of the Holy Spirit upon individuals and upon the church in general; and it is in order that we may be clear about this that we should consider this question of gifts. Obviously, if the Spirit chooses to give them, it is a wonderful attestation of the truth. But it remains in his sovereignty and we must not lay down any rules of our own.

Are we to assume, then, that everything that claims to be a reappearance or a revival of such gifts in the church is of necessity true? That is the immediate and urgent practical question. We are open; we have no longer shut our minds to the possibility in terms of a false understanding of the scriptural teaching; we are clear about that. And suddenly we hear reports of the appearance of the gifts. Are we therefore to accept them immediately as being the gifts and the manifestations of the Holy Spirit?

At this point there are two main dangers which confront us. The first is the danger of quenching the Spirit. I put that first because I believe it is the more common of the two. There are people who automatically discount anything that is reported; their whole bias of mind, their whole prejudice is against it. History demonstrates that the greatest opposition to a true revival in the church, or to the work of individual men who have been baptized with the Spirit, has almost invariably come from the church herself. It is a startling, frightening truth, and it is all due to quenching the Spirit. The Roman Catholic Church persecuted the Reformers for this very reason; and, alas, the Protestant Church has often in her turn persecuted men upon whom the Spirit of God has come.

Why? Well, the danger is institutionalism and the fondness for decorum, order and pomp and ceremony with everything being controlled and ordered. So that if anything different happens it is immediately frowned upon and disliked. It is the same as the objection to the personal emphasis in the gospel. I have quoted elsewhere that remark of Lord Melbourne, Queen Victoria's first Prime Minister, who said, 'Things are coming to a pretty pass if religion is going to start becoming personal.' How typical that is! We want a dignified religion which never disturbs us, nor anybody else. There must be no liberty and freedom of the Spirit—the very thought is almost indecent. Fancy upsetting the clock-like, mechanical perfection of a great service with an outpouring of the Spirit! The thing is unthinkable! Now that is quenching the Spirit, and so you find the Apostle saying, 'Quench not the Spirit.'

Temperament undoubtedly comes into this. Some people have the temperament which leads to their liking order and discipline and decorum and so on; and they have to watch that. Their danger is to quench the Spirit, and this is a very real danger. And so there are many people in the Christian church who, the moment they hear of anything unusual, condemn it. 'There must not be anything unusual. We have never had anything like this before,' they say. That has always been the opposition to revival; that is why the saints have always been persecuted by people who like the ordinary, the drab, the uneventful and the dead. And remember it can be true of orthodox people quite as much as others. You can have a dead orthodoxy as well as a dead formality. The great danger confronting the majority is that of quenching and resisting the Spirit, thereby standing against the sovereignty of the Holy Spirit.

The other danger is the exact opposite and it is interesting to see how the one extreme or the other predominates: it is the danger of an uncritical acceptance of everything. Again temperament comes into this. Some people are credulous. It is very interesting reading the history of the church to see this element coming out in some of God's great servants. There are some men who are always anxious for the unusual—it is the thing they have to watch. Each of us has got to know himself or herself. We all have certain weaknesses and tendencies and we must watch them. It is the most difficult thing in the world: 'Know thyself!' And we have to be on our guard lest our natural temperament should become a prejudice and we may be found fighting against God.

This uncritical acceptance is often the result of a spirit of fear. You see, the first people are never afraid of quenching the Spirit at all; they just have their set fixed opinion in which everything different is condemned. But then there is this other type, who are terrified of quenching the Spirit. And that can become 'a spirit of fear' which interferes with their critical faculties, so that they are ready to believe anything and everything. They are so afraid of standing against a work of God that they pass things that they should not pass.

This, of course, is what always leads to fanaticism, or what the Bible calls a false fire. Here again not only does the Bible give us great teaching, but history also confirms the danger of fanaticism, wild fire, of another spirit simulating the Holy Spirit. Fanaticism is always to be condemned and it has often caused great havoc in the life of the church. Even an uncritical acceptance of anything purported to be the manifestation of the gifts of the Spirit may well lead to manifestations of certain excesses. Again, anybody who has ever read the history of revivals will know this danger and also that of a false emphasis, a lack of balance, the kind of thing that was obviously happening in the church at Corinth and which necessitated that section which the great Apostle devotes to it.

We proceed now to the next big principle. Why must we not accept uncritically everything that claims to be a manifestation of the power of the Holy Spirit? The answer is, first and foremost, that the Scriptures themselves warn us against uncritically accepting everything that is put before us. This is for the simple reason that there is such a being and person as the devil, that there are such entities as evil spirits, foul and malign spirits. You remember the great word of the apostle in Ephesians 6:12, 'For we wrestle not against flesh and blood, but against principalities, against powers, against the rulers of the darkness of this world, against spiritual wickedness in high places.' The beginning of this matter is to realize that we are living in a spiritual realm, a spiritual atmosphere. This world is not only a material one—there is the spiritual element surrounding it and there are forces and spirits which are evil and malign, set against God and everything that is holy. That is why by contrast the third person in the Trinity is designated the 'holy' Spirit.

If we do not begin by realizing that there are these two kinds of spiritual powers and forces, we are doomed to disaster because the teaching of Scripture is that these evil powers and spirits are always there and they have tremendous power. You see it even in the Old Testament. You remember how Moses, the servant of God, was given power in order that he might have means to attest his claim to his

God-given leadership. He was sent by God to rescue the children of Israel, but Moses foresaw the difficulty. He said in effect, 'When I go and say this to them they will turn to me and they will say, Who are you, why should we listen to you? You are asking us to take a great risk. All right, said God, I will tell you . . . . I will tell you what to say . . . . say that I AM has sent me'. But God said beyond that, 'Look at that staff you have in your hand; I will enable you to do things through that.' He gave him certain miraculous powers. But that alone, you remember, was not sufficient, because the magicians of Egypt were able to repeat and to counterfeit many of the things that were done by Moses. So the apostle Paul, in writing his second letter to Timothy, referring to those magicians, and comparing them with the evil teachers of his day, says, 'As Jannes and Jambres withstood Moses, so do these also resist the truth: men of corrupt minds, reprobate concerning the faith' (2 Tim 3:8). There, then, we have a great instance of this very thing in the Old Testament.

Unfortunately, things are not, therefore, quite as simple as some people seem to think. We are always surrounded by these evil spirits as well as by the 'holy' Spirit and their one object is to ruin the work of God. The devil rebelled against God, and his great ambition is to bring God's work into disrepute. There is nothing that he is more ready to do, therefore, than to confuse Christian people, especially those who are most spiritual, and the havoc that the devil has wrought in the history of the church is quite appalling to consider. Because of this, Scripture not only gives us the history and its teaching about the devil and his followers, but it also goes so far as to tell us to 'try the spirits', to 'prove the spirits'. 'Try the spirits whether they are of God', says John in his first epistle chapter 4:1. Now that is a commandment. 'Believe not every spirit', he says. Do not believe every spirit, but prove them and try them to see whether they are of God, or 'of the world' as he puts it, and that is an actual injunction to us. We are not therefore to accept everything that is reported. No; the Bible tells us to exercise our critical faculties and to prove and test them.

Writing to the Thessalonian church, Paul says, 'Prove all things; hold fast that which is good' (1 Thess 5:21). Do you notice the context? He started by saying, 'Quench not the Spirit'. There is the rebuke to that first group—do not quench the Spirit. There were people who were doing that, but you must not, says Paul. But then, he says, do not go to the other extreme, 'Prove all things.' Do not be uncritical because I have told you not to quench the Spirit and not to despise prophesying. Do not act hastily and say, 'All right, I will believe everything. . . .' 'Prove all things; only hold fast to that which is good.' You will have to reject a lot, but 'Hold fast to that which is good.' Now there it is as plain as anything could be.

Let me sum up this point by putting it like this. The trouble in the church at Corinth was entirely due to their failure to do this very thing that the Apostle exhorts the churches to do. They were confused about spiritual things because they had not learnt this all-important lesson.

In addition to Scripture we have exactly the same warning from the history of the Christian church—and you notice that I keep on putting these two things together. We must do so. The church is one. The church is the church of God, and essentially the same throughout the ages. There is an amazing continuity, and the principles taught in Scripture are worked out in the history of the church. And because we are in the flesh, we are helped by examples and illustrations, hence the great value of history. I know of nothing next to the reading of the Scriptures themselves that has been of greater value to me in my own personal life and ministry than constant reading of the history of the church. I thank

God for it more than ever, for the way in which, by illustrating these things, it has saved me from pitfalls and has shown me the right way to assess these matters.

So we turn to history and we find that very early in the Christian church great difficulties arose owing to this very matter. This is a very difficult subject. There was a movement towards the middle of the second century called Montanism. I want to be careful about this because I believe that Montanism has been wrongly judged on many occasions. The official church was against it, because the official church was tending to become institutional and the Montanists were concerned about life and power. But there is no doubt that the Montanists went too far in this; they violated certain biblical principles such as, that women should not be teachers in the church, and that in itself showed that they had already gone wrong somewhere. And with that certain excesses tended to come in at the same time.

Then as you come on down the centuries you will find that the Roman Catholic Church began to report almost endless miracles; they began doing this in the fourth century. And, of course, it increased by leaps and bounds. They were claiming the most amazing miracles—healings and various other forms of miracles. Generally they happened in connection with what are called the 'relics of saints'. A bone was claimed to be from the body of Peter or some other 'saint' and this had miraculous qualities; or it was the 'grave' of a saint, or some such site, where endless miracles were reported. You will even find great men like Saint Augustine and Chrysostom and others reporting them and believing in them; by the Middle Ages it had become not only widespread but very profitable for the church herself.

What are called the miracles of the Roman Catholic Church, such as you get at Lourdes at the present time, are another fact and phenomenon in connection with the history of the church. Many people—credulous, uncritical people—are prepared to believe any wonder or sign by which they may be confronted and immediately to attribute it to the work of the Holy Spirit. Many people have done this and become 'converts to Rome', directly as the result of this kind of thing. There, then, is one great warning from history. We shall be dealing with these things again later on.

Coming down the centuries you find the same thing in Protestantism. It is very interesting when reading about the great Revival of two hundred years ago, connected with men such as Whitefield and the Wesleys, to consider the story of what were called 'The French Prophets', particularly in London. Many of the Huguenots had come over to this country at the end of the seventeenth century and this kind of connection was kept up. There had been certain phenomena in some parts of France and they gradually came over to this country. It is very interesting to notice how even a discriminating, intellectual man like John Wesley, was for a while captivated by this. Whitefield was not, as he was always more fearful of these matters. But John Wesley, who for so long had clung to his own intellect and understanding, tended as such men often do to swing too far to the other extreme. He became credulous and was greatly impressed by the manifestations of these so-called French prophets. But eventually he came to see that at the very least it was very doubtful whether all these manifestations were of the Spirit of God and not rather of the evil spirit.

In other words, I am simply trying to make this point. You hear a great deal at the present time about the revival of these gifts and so on, but this is not the first time this has been reported, nor the first time it has been claimed. It is a repetition of something that has happened frequently in the history of the church.

Let me move on to the last century and to the whole

episode known under the name of Irvingism, in connection with Edward Irving. This mas was a brilliant Scot, a one time assistant to the great Dr Thomas Chalmers, who subsequently came down to London and began to preach in the Scottish Church near Hatton Garden. He became the sensation of London in the 1820s. People flocked to hear him, including society people. He had many things which attracted—his personality, his appearance, eloquence and so on—and he became one of the most popular men in the whole of London. But the story ended in great tragedy and it all arose from the claim that the gifts of the Holy Spirit were being renewed and were being repeated under his ministry. I must not take you through the history; there are books which have been written on this, which are most instructive to read. But I have had the privilege of reading a little booklet called *Narrative of Events* by Robert Baxter, which I should like to refer to at this point.

Robert Baxter was a barrister who lived in Doncaster. He was an able, godly, spiritually minded man, who for a while became the very centre of the movement round Edward Irving, and their leading prophet. He claimed to be receiving messages direct from God, messages concerning the truth to be delivered, and what he was to do. He was told, he claimed, by the Spirit of God that he must leave his wife and family and his profession, and go and deliver this message. He was told, he claimed further, to go into the law courts and to get up and interrupt a case and address the judge and deliver this message from the Spirit of God, if he felt the impulse while he sat in court. Actually he did not feel the impulse, and did not do this, but he had taken steps to leave his wife and family, having been told that he was not to bid them farewell even, but was to go at once.

All this was reported and was regarded as the leading of the Spirit. Men claimed to be speaking in other tongues and

Robert Baxter, who was at the very heart and centre of this, was regarded as an 'oracle', as an unusually spirited man. He testified that his love of the Lord was greater than ever and so was his happiness. Yet this man came to see that all this was not of the Spirit of God. Exact prophecies had been given to him but they were not verified, and did not happen. And then he began to realize that some of these things he was told to do were not in accord with the plain teaching of Scripture. But he had thought, and he was as honest as the day, that this was all the Spirit of God. Eventually his understanding was restored to him and he continued the rest of his life a godly, saintly man in the church. It was to warn others that he wrote that book long since out of print called *Narrative of Events.*

Now, my dear friends, we must not discount such things. Irvingism collapsed, though they did establish what they called the Catholic Apostolic Church. But the whole thing ended in disaster, including the death of poor Irving who was overwrought and even suffered physically, eventually dying a broken man. There were certain prophetesses who even denounced one another while some of them later admitted and confessed that they had invented facts at certain points. Do not misunderstand me—I am not saying all this in order that you may say the moment you hear of any claim, 'Obviously nonsense! A repetition of Irvingism; have nothing to do with it.' That is not my object. All I am saying is do not believe everything uncritically. 'Prove all things; hold fast that which is good.'

I could recount at length stories about the freak religious sects that arose in the United States in the last century. A book was written once on these called *Group Movements and Experiments in Guidance.* Now the point about them all is that there was no doubt about their sincerity. They all really believed that the things they experienced were the acts of the Spirit of God, but the story ends in disaster.

Let me move on to a third bit of evidence which is equally important and which illustrates the danger of evil spirits counterfeiting to mislead 'if it were possible even the very elect'. The third evidence is that from spiritism and from psychology. Here again the thing is quite clear if you take the trouble to examine it. I have never understood those people who say that all that is claimed for spiritism should be rejected. A man like the late Sir Oliver Lodge was not a fool, neither was the late Sir Arthur Conan Doyle. I know that there is a lot of dishonesty in the realm of spiritism and a lot of fictitious evidence has often been presented. But—and I think that the Society for Psychical Research has established this—there is always a residuum which simply cannot be explained away in terms of trickery and dishonesty. There are such things as phenomena belonging to spiritism. I have no difficulty in believing this, because I believe the whole of spiritism is the manifestation of the work of evil spirits. There are evil spirits who can produce phenomena and can do amazing things.

In other words there is no question—and it has been reported and established many times over—that in spiritism you have people who can speak in tongues. Evil spirits can make people speak in strange tongues and languages that people do not understand. They can counterfeit the speaking in tongues produced by the Holy Spirit. To all appearances they appear to be identical. Not only that, but there is no question that healings can happen in the realm of spiritism. This again has been checked by careful observers and people who do not believe in spiritism at all. You cannot say that the whole of the work of a man like the famous Harry Edwards is all dishonesty and fraud. There are certain cases of healings which are as genuine as anything that can be reported by Christian faith healers. It is ridiculous to deny the facts. The danger is that the practitioner claims that he is the medium of the spirit of a dead person.

I am putting this evidence before you as a warning—spiritist phenomena can be amazingly like these other phenomena, so that if you are going to believe anything that is put before you uncritically, you are obviously exposing yourself to the deceit of spiritism and all that belongs to that realm.

This is, also, true of psychology. All this is being discovered more and more and it is receiving a good deal of attention of course. You may have seen programmes on the television, or read the book by Dr William Sargent, *Battle for the Mind* where the intention is to discount the Christian faith and to explain it all away in terms of psychology. What they can demonstrate is that under hypnotism you can make people speak in other languages which they know nothing about and of which they have never heard. And there are people who can hypnotize themselves and make themselves do this without invoking the spiritual realm at all. Purely on the level of psychology, you can reproduce certain spiritual phenomena, such as speaking in tongues by auto-suggestion and auto-hypnosis or by the reviving of something that is deep down and lost in the memory, something of which the man is no longer conscious can be brought to the surface again. There are extraordinary phenomena along that line.

Then there is the whole realm of hysteria where almost anything can happen. You will hear people say, 'Now look, if you are going to base your Christianity upon the presence of these phenomena, here they are for you,' and they will produce them by using hypnotism, hysteria and trance conditions. They will give you pictures which they have taken in certain odd sects in various parts of the world where you can see the thing happening psychologically. There it is, they say, and that is the whole of your Christianity—Christianity is nothing but that.

These are some of the reasons why you and I must pay close heed to the exhortations of Scripture. 'Prove the spirits'; 'test the spirits'; 'prove all things; hold fast only to that which is good'. It is our bounden duty as we value the doctrine of God and as we are concerned about the state of the church. God forbid that people should confuse the phenomena, the manifestations, with the baptism of the Spirit itself, because if they do people who reject the phenomena will reject the baptism with the Spirit also. These two things must be kept distinct and separate.

How do we test the spirits? It is vital that we should know how to test, especially those of us who really know something of the burden of the times in which we live. God forbid that there should be anybody sitting back in smug satisfaction and contentment at this point and saying, 'Of course, at last he has said it, I have been waiting for it all the while. I have always said there is nothing in this, lot of nonsense—some even say it is of the devil.' God have mercy upon you if you can be smug in the Christian church at a time like this!

No, I am speaking particularly to those good, honest, spiritually-minded men and women of any age whatsoever, who are longing for revival and reawakening, longing to see the church speaking with power in this evil age, addressing governments if necessary, doing something that will arrest the moral declension that is happening round and about us and believing that this is what we need. It is to such people that I address these words in particular. For it is your very anxiety to know the fullness and the baptism of the Spirit that constitutes your danger and exposes you to this possibility of not using your critical faculties as you should.

At this point I will give you the negative only: Do not rely only upon your inward feelings. Many have done this and have found themselves in grievous difficulty. What I mean is that they make decisions entirely on their own inner feeling. They say, 'You know, I have a feeling that this is right. I don't like that other possibility.' But that is entirely subjective, and while I do not discount the subjective altogether, I say it is not enough. You must not rely solely upon some inner inward sense, because that is the very thing the devil wants you to do. That means you are not using your full critical faculties; deciding in a purely emotional and subjective manner.

Let me add this: do not be swayed even by the fact that something reported to you makes you feel wonderful. You may say, 'Well now surely anything that makes me feel greater love to God must be right.' Robert Baxter, to whom I have already referred in connection with the Irvingite movement, used to say that he had never felt so much love, the love of God in his heart, or so much love in himself to God as he did at this period. He was ready to leave his wife and family for God's sake. He was filled with a sense of the love of God, he said, that he had never known before, but he came to see that it had all been misleading him.

So we must not judge even in terms of such feelings. You may say, 'I have never known such love, I have never known such peace, I have never known such joy.' The people who belong to the cults will often tell you exactly the same thing. So we must not rely upon our own subjective feelings. Do not dismiss them or discount them, but do not rely upon them. Do not say, 'I feel this is right, everything in me says this is right, all my Christian spirit.' It is not enough. The devil is as subtle as that. Remember our Lord's word—'if it were possible, they shall deceive the very elect.'

Lastly, do not base your judgement on the people who are speaking to you and making their report to you. The tendency is to say, 'Well now, I know this man to be a good

Christian man, an honest soul, and a most devout person—therefore anything he says must be right.' He may be wrong! He is not perfect, the devil has brought down greater and stronger men than he. So the mere fact that the report is brought to you by good people who may say to you, 'My whole experience has been transformed by this', is not enough. It may be right, it may be wrong.

Once again, you have these warnings not only in Scripture but in the continuing history of the Christian church. It is often some of the best, most honest and sincere people who can be most seriously led astray. The cynics sit back and say, 'Of course, I knew that that was false.' Exactly! They say that about everything. They say that about the true as well as the false. They down everything, they condemn everything. God have mercy upon them. Are they Christian at all, I wonder? No, it is the good and the honest and the true soul that the devil tempts most of all because this person is the nearest to the Lord. The devil does not waste any of his time and energy with your smug formalist—he is safely asleep, already under the drug of the devil, though he is sitting in a Christian church. The devil does not waste time with him. But the man about whom he really is concerned is the man who is anxious to follow his Lord all the way.

So I say that you must not decide merely in terms of the character of the people giving the report, nor even in terms of their experience, whatever they may say to you. Be open, be ready to listen but never be uncritical, 'Prove all things; hold fast that which is good.'

Chapter 4

Understanding and the Word

As we resume our studies, I would again remind you that our reason for looking into this great matter of the baptism with the Holy Spirit and the gifts of the Spirit is not *only* that it is in the Scriptures. It is our business always to investigate and to study everything that is in the Scriptures; we do not pick and choose. If we believe that this is the word of God, well it is all the word of God and we are to be familiar with the teaching of the entire Bible. We have no right to ignore teaching simply because we do not happen to like it or because we think it may involve us in difficulties and problems. That is the first and main reason for studying this subject.

But in addition the whole state and condition of the Christian church at the present time makes this study imperative. We are witnessing a world in sin and chaos, and it is surely by now evident to everybody that nothing but a great outpouring of the Spirit of God upon the church can be of any avail in such a situation. We have tried everything else, and I am not disparaging the efforts of men, but it is quite clear that human organizations and attempts are really not touching the true situation as it exists in this and in other lands. God's method throughout the centuries has been to send a revival among his people, to pour out his Spirit again upon his church. For this reason, it is urgently important for us to examine the teaching concerning this and to look at it especially in the light of the subsequent history of the church. And so we will continue our study of the gifts of the Spirit.

In our last study we began to consider how we should test the phenomena and I offered the negative advice not to trust feelings. Now I should like to consider the positive ways of testing and examining each phenomenon. Firstly, we should use our reason and understanding. Now some may be surprised that I start with this and not with the Scriptures. My reason for doing so, of course, is that in the early church they did not have the Scriptures as we have them. The question arises: how could they test? How could they prove the spirits? So I start with reason and understanding and this, I think, is a most important matter. Let me show you what I mean. I would lay down as a proposition to be found in the Scriptures themselves that we must never abandon or jettison our minds, our reason, our understanding. Let me put it in the phrase that is most commonly used. We must never 'let ourselves go'.

Those of you who are interested in these matters, and especially in the new interest that is being taken in these things at the present time in this country, in America and in other parts of the world, will know exactly what I mean. There is a teaching which comes to us and says, 'Now if you want this blessing, let yourself go, and especially your mind .... If you want this you have got to abandon yourself, to let yourself go.'

I am trying to show that that is always wrong, but I want to make this point clear. Someone may say to me, 'But surely you are contradicting the plain teaching of the Scriptures, which you yourself are never tired of emphasizing, namely, that a man does not reason himself into Christianity, that a man by mere intellectual understanding and effort will never make himself a Christian', to which the answer is quite simple —that is perfectly right. We never can 'reason' ourselves into Christianity. We can never by means of an intellectual process bring ourselves into the truth and into the kingdom of God. That is true. But it is equally important that we should remember that Christianity is not unreasonable and never irrational—never! You cannot reason yourself into it, but the moment you are in it you find that it is the most reasonable and rational thing of all.

At no point, then, are we deliberately to abandon our intellects. There is never instruction in the Scriptures for us to do that. Deliberately to stop thinking and to let ourselves become blank, as it were, and to surrender ourselves to other forces—that is never advocated in the Scriptures. How, then, does one become a Christian? It happens like this: the Holy Spirit enlightens the understanding. He does not make us Christians apart from the understanding. What he does is to lift the understanding up to a higher level. There is nothing wrong with reason except that it is governed by a sinful disposition, and that is why it can never bring us into Christianity or into the kingdom. But the Spirit can lift up the mind and the reason. A man is never saved against his reason and his understanding—never! What happens is that his understanding and his reason are enabled to see the truth which he formerly rejected. 'But the natural man,' says the Apostle, 'receiveth not the things of the Spirit of God: for they are foolishness unto him: neither can he know them, because they are spiritually discerned.' Quite right. But the answer is not to commit intellectual suicide, nor to stop thinking, nor deliberately to let yourself go and abandon the powers that God has given you. The answer is to trust yourself to the illumination and the guidance of the

Spirit. As you do that so the Spirit will illumine the mind. As the Apostle puts it in 1 Corinthians 2:10—'But God hath revealed them unto us by his Spirit: for the Spirit searcheth all things, yea, the deep things of God.'

I trust this point is clear. Intellect alone cannot enable us to grasp the truth, but when the revelation is given through the Spirit, the intellect and the reason do grasp the truth, rejoice in it and apprehend it.

There is my first answer to this, but let me give you a second one which is still more important. The whole presupposition behind the argument in 1 Corinthians chapters 12, 13 and 14 is the exercise of the understanding, and reason, and that is the same with all the other New Testament teaching. Why was the church at Corinth in trouble over the exercise and manifestation of these gifts? Because they were not employing their reason and their understanding, they were abandoning themselves.

Let me work this out with you. Take that injunction in the first epistle of John: 'Beloved, believe not every spirit, but try the spirits whether they are of God: because many false prophets are gone out into the world' (1 Jn 4:1). Now how can you possibly prove or try the spirits unless you are using your mind and reason and understanding? The thing is impossible. The position represented is this. Here is man with the Holy Spirit on the one side and the evil spirits, and the spirit of antichrist on the other side, and they are both trying to possess us and to influence us. How do we know which is which? If you 'abandon' yourself, or let yourself go, or stop thinking, or cease to reason and apply your understanding, how can you test? It is impossible! And it is because they were not doing that, or refusing to do that, that trouble arose in the church at Corinth.

But there is another way in which we can look at this. In 1 Corinthians 14 the Apostle deals—and I hope to come back to this later—with the whole question of the misuse of the gift of speaking in tongues. They were tending to misuse it or at any rate wanting to exercise it the whole time when they gathered together, and so the Apostle warns them of the effect that would have on a possible outsider coming in: 'If therefore the whole church be come together into one place, and all speak with tongues, and there come in those that are unlearned, or unbelievers, will they not say that ye are mad?' (1 Cor 14:23). Now that is the position that the Apostle had to deal with. The Corinthians wanted to spend the whole of the time in their church meetings in speaking in tongues that other people could not understand.

Now what is the Apostle's advice to them, what is his exhortation and his teaching? It is that this must be controlled, and that you cannot at one and the same time abandon yourself, let yourself go, and still be in control. The verse which puts it all in a nutshell is 1 Corinthians 14:32—'And the spirits of the prophets are subject to the prophets.' Now that settles it surely once and for ever! You are not to let yourself go, because if you do, you will expose yourself to the other spirits, you will not be able to test, and still more, you will not be able to control. So Paul ends that chapter with the injunction: 'Let all things be done decently and in order', which is impossible if you abandon your thinking, your reason, and your understanding.

Now there is a problem here and I am going to deal with it later on. It is to me one of the most wonderful aspects of this truth—how at one and the same time you can be gripped and lifted up by the Spirit and still be in control. But that is the glory of Christianity, that is what differentiates it from everything that is false and spurious. So I argue that the first thing we have to do is to use our reason and understanding, the very powers that God has given us. Indeed I want to put this as a positive assertion, that it is the very central glory of the Christian salvation that it takes up the whole man. It takes up his mind, his heart and his will. Any teaching that tells you that you are only going to get the blessing if you stop thinking is contrary to the teaching of the gospel itself. Here is something that enlightens the eyes of our understanding. The mind is at full stretch, the intellect is involved, it is taken up and the whole man is involved.

So, then, we are right to be suspicious of anything that tries either by its methods or by suggestion to stop us thinking. I mean by that the employment of certain well-known psychological techniques such as putting out the lights and having a rhythmic repetition of music or of phrases. You must have seen and read about the kind of thing that happens amongst the more primitive races, how they slowly work themselves up by these means into a condition in which they are no longer thinking and have lost the power of reasoning and understanding. Anything that does that should be suspect. There is nothing approaching it in the New Testament, indeed you find the exact opposite.

What is this message which we believe? Well it is called the truth, and that is patently something that comes primarily to a man's mind; so that any suggestion that you 'let yourself go' already indicates that there are at the least very good grounds for suspecting such a teaching.

Let us now move on to the second great principle as to how we should test the spirits and that is the Scriptures themselves. I have already reminded you that the early church had not got the Scriptures as we have them. The churches were in being, these problems had already arisen and that is why the apostles had to write their letters. But these people were obviously in a position, before that, to apply certain tests. But today, thank God, we have the Scriptures and it is therefore our business to use them. 'The church,' says the Apostle Paul, 'is built upon the foundation of the apostles and prophets' (Eph 2:20) and it is through these men that we have the Scriptures. Here is authoritative teaching—here is all the teaching that we need. There is no need of a supplement to the Scriptures, because everything we need has already been given to us here.

Now we shall consider the way in which we should apply these tests. We must realize that there is no greater danger than that of putting the Spirit against the Scriptures. All who are at all familiar with the history of the church will know exactly what I mean. This is always the characteristic of the false movements, of heresies if you like; especially those that are concerned with spiritual gifts and manifestations. They always tend to put the Spirit against the word, and eventually arrive at a position where they do not hesitate to say that the Scriptures are no longer necessary. Why, they ask, do you need the Scriptures if you have got the inner light? If you are receiving direct messages from the Spirit, where is the need of the Scriptures?

This is a most important matter and it is one of the first tests that we must apply to anything that offers itself to us as a new manifestation of the Holy Spirit, particularly in this matter of gifts. Watch the place that is given to the Scriptures. You will often find in the history of such movements that, while they start well, there is an increasing tendency on their part to use Scripture less and less and to attach greater and greater significance to what they call 'prophetic messages'. They talk more about them, pay more attention to them, and begin to print them instead of expositions of the word of God; that is always a most dangerous sign.

In Scripture is all the truth we need, and what we need is the illumination of the Holy Spirit upon our minds to enable us to understand it and to expound it. So I would lay it down as a valuable and general rule, that if you see an increasing tendency to base a position less and less upon the Scriptures, and to spend less and less time in expounding them, but more and more time in what are claimed to be direct messages from the Spirit, then you are entitled to have all your suspicions aroused and it is your duty to be on guard.

Again I can illustrate this quite simply from the history of the church. There were movements that arose in the early church, that is in the first three centuries, which fell into this very error. It was one of the great dangers with Montanism and other similar movements. But perhaps one of the most striking examples of this was immediately after the Protestant Reformation. For centuries the Roman Catholic Church had been governing everything with its iron, rigid system, and its own interpretation of the Scriptures. The Protestant Reformers saw through that error. They grasped the whole truth of the universal priesthood of all believers; they saw that every man with the Spirit is entitled to come and to read the Scriptures, and people were liberated as the result of that. But, you see, the enemy came in and tried to press this too far to the other extreme. The exact opposite of Roman Catholicism, in a sense, is what is called the Anabaptist movement. You can read about the movements which arose in the sixteenth century and which caused such trouble to people like Martin Luther, Zwingli, John Calvin and others.

Let me say quite frankly that I think those great Protestant Reformers were too severe on them and went astray themselves in their condemnation; but what they were facing was the danger that these wild movements—which said you did not need the Scriptures at all, that the Spirit gave you direct guidance on everything—were likely to wreck the Reformation altogether; they put the Catholics into the position of being able to say, 'The moment you leave us what do you get?—chaos and utter confusion.' So it is interesting to see how these men calling themselves 'prophets', claimed, not so much that they were expounding the Scriptures, but that they had immediate and direct guidance.

A still more well-known example, of course, is that of the Quakers. George Fox and others started with the Scriptures, and all they claimed was that they had the light within them to enable them to understand. But very soon they had left that position and were saying more or less that you did not need Scriptures at all. You had this inner light or guidance and all you did was to look to the Spirit and he would tell you. And so they increasingly turned their backs upon the Scriptures, and that has persisted as a characteristic of that movement even until today.

You find the same thing in the history of Irvingism, to which I have already referred. They again left the Scriptures and looked more and more to these prophetic utterances. When Robert Baxter was present, all they did was to sit and listen to what he had to say claiming, as he did, to be speaking under the power and the influence of the Spirit, and getting a direct message. He did not preach, or expound the Scriptures, but just gave these prophetic messages, as they were called. And, as I reminded you, it not only led to confusion but finally it ended in tragedy and Baxter himself came to see that it was not the Spirit of God at all as he had thought, and he was mercifully restored to a Christian and scriptural position.

These, then, are the two main principles involved in testing the spirits. We must use our minds and our understanding, and must never 'let ourselves go'. We must not abandon ourselves for in doing so we lose the ability to be critical, to evaluate, to prove and to control. Above all, we must apply the Scriptures. We have the Spirit in us, our mind is enlightened and we have the Scriptures. We must put these things together. Nothing is more dangerous than to put a wedge between the word and the Spirit, to emphasize either one at the expense of the other. It is the Spirit *and* the word, the

Spirit *upon* the word, and the Spirit in us as we read the word.

How do we carry out these principles in detail? I am going to put before you a number of general principles which seem to me to be helpful. I put them forward as the result of reading the Scriptures, together with my own experience over the years. They are also the result of my reading of church history and of movements in connection with the life of the church. Here are some of the conclusions at which I have arrived and which I would put to you as general principles which you can apply.

To begin with, always be suspicious of—indeed, I would go further and say, be ready to condemn and to reject—anything that claims to be a fresh revelation of truth.

I am sure you know what I mean by that. People in this state and condition claim that something has been revealed to them. There are certain well-known movements, even at this present time, which were started by people claiming to have had a special revelation.

One of the most common revelations of all concerns the second coming of our blessed Lord and Saviour. They claim that it has been revealed to them that our Lord is coming again in a given year. Seventh Day Adventism, as it is called, started in that way. A man called Russell and a woman called Mrs Eleanor White claimed that the Holy Spirit had revealed directly to them the exact year when our Lord was going to come. It did not happen of course, but it does not matter and the movement goes on. The point I am establishing is that the whole thing was based upon what is claimed to have been a direct and immediate revelation concerning a particular truth.

How do you test a thing like that? What do you say if someone comes to you and says that it has been revealed to them, in a spiritual state, that the Lord is going to return, let us say in 1970?* Well, I suggest that what you should *not* do is to start working through the figures and the numerics of the Scriptures, which so many do. I should have thought that it is quite sufficient to take just one scripture which tells you that you are not to be concerned about the times and seasons; and, therefore, if you are given an exact date you should reply that the Bible tells us that we are not to know the exact date: 'But of the times and the seasons, brethren, ye have no need that I write unto you'. Why? Well you know that the Lord will so come 'as a thief in the night' (2 Pet 3:10). Our Lord himself said when he was in this world that even he did not know the exact date, that it was only known to God. Therefore this is a claim to a fresh revelation and it is contrary to scriptural teaching. You are entitled on those grounds alone to reject it.

But, alas, people have not done this. They have said, 'but look at this person, this Mrs White, what a godly woman she was,' and there have been others who have claimed exactly the same thing. In connection with the Irving movement again, there was great concentration on the second coming —indeed it was the very centre of the teaching that seems to have been particularly popular in America and in this country just at that time.

But let me give you a still more interesting illustration of this, one which is not so well known. There has been a teaching which has gained great popularity in evangelical circles, concerning what is known as 'the secret rapture of the saints'. It teaches that the Lord at his second coming will appear only to his saints, and that they will be raptured into the heavens secretly with nobody seeing it, nobody knowing anything at all about it; all they will know is that suddenly the saints will have gone.

I wonder whether you know the history and the story of

* These sermons were preached in 1965.

that teaching? The people who hold it seem to assume that this has always been the teaching of the church, that it is truly biblical teaching, but do you know its history? The answer is that this teaching was first put forward in 1830. It had never been heard of before.

How then did it start? The answer is most interesting; again we must bring in the name of Edward Irving. In about 1830 the people who had become known as the Plymouth Brethren, including such names as J.N. Darby, B.W. Newton and S.P.Tregelles, and others of the early first leaders of the Brethren movement, began to gather together with Edward Irving and some of his followers to hold what they called Prophetic Conferences. They became interested in the whole doctrine of our Lord's second coming, and they said, 'This has been neglected and we must look into it and we must examine it.' So they held conferences at a place called Powerscourt. And it was in connection with those conferences that this whole idea of the secret rapture of the saints came in. We have the authority of S.P. Tregelles, a great and famous biblical scholar, who tells us how it happened in a book he wrote called *The Hope of Christ's Second Coming*. In it he says, 'I am not aware that there was any definite teaching that there should be a secret rapture of the Church at a secret Coming until this was given forth as an "utterance" [notice his inverted commas] in Mr. Irving's church from what was then received as being the voice of the Spirit. But whether anyone ever asserted such a thing or not it was from that supposed revelation that the modern doctrine and the modern phraseology respecting it arose.' Tragelles attended these conferences, so he speaks with authority.

In Edward Irving's church they claimed that the gifts of the Spirit had all been restored, prophetic utterances among them, and it was through one of these supposed utterances of the Spirit that this idea of the secret rapture of the saints came in. So this was something that they claimed the Spirit had given as a direct revelation, and they accepted it. What is amazing is that a man like J.N. Darby accepted it, but he did, and he continued to teach it, and it has been taught very commonly ever since then. Tregelles would not accept it, neither would B.W. Newton. It was the first cause of a division amongst the Plymouth Brethren. (Incidentally, J.N. Darby very soon saw the dangerous tendencies in Edward Irving and entirely broke with him, but he continued to accept the secret rapture solely as the result of what claimed to be a prophetic utterance.)

The principle I am laying down, therefore, is that one should be most cautious in accepting anything that claims to be a new teaching or a fresh or additional revelation. That should always be regarded with the profoundest suspicion, because, as I say, it is unnecessary, and because so often you will find that it contradicts something that is clearly taught in the Scripture itself. That leads us to a second principle. Obviously, if what someone claims is a message from the Spirit, contradicts quite patently a teaching of the Scripture, again you reject it.

Let me illustrate what I mean by this. It is quite astonishing to notice the credulity of people, including Christians, which leads them to expose themselves either to charlatans or to men who are mentally deranged. I referred earlier to a book reprinted in the 1930s called *Group Movements and Experiments in Guidance*, which is an illuminating account of various freak religious movements in the United States in the last century. Now is it credible to you that sane Christians, godly spiritual people could accept a thing like this. A certain teacher claimed that he was so filled with the Spirit that you had only to touch him in order to receive a blessing. We read in Acts 19 of special miracles wrought by the Apostle Paul, whereby if sick people sent their handkerchiefs and put them on Paul's body they could be healed by putting those handkerchiefs on their own bodies. So those Christians applied that and said, 'Yes, this man is the same.' They thought he had been so filled with the Spirit that just physical contact with him would give the blessing. So people went in large numbers in order to do this. It ended in a most tragic manner. I think the man was mentally deranged, but it ended in his claiming that this blessing was obtained at its maximum if people actually slept with him in the same bed. I need say no more. Both men and women did that and it ended, of course, in a grave scandal.

The point I am trying to establish, my dear friends, is simply that this was a trap into which good, godly, spiritually-minded people fell, people who really wanted the full blessing of God. Of course, the formal church members did not fall into the trap; they just sat back and said, 'We told you so, every time you get this talk about the Spirit that is where it is going to end.' God have mercy upon them! God have mercy upon them! It is better to be too credulous than to be carnal and to be smug and dead. No, this is something, I say, that constitutes a danger to the best people. For the moment you abandon your tests and let yourself go, the moment you stop thinking, 'Where is there anything like that in the Scriptures', you fall a prey to such things as I have just quoted.

Let me give you another example. I personally have known at least two ministers, who as the result of great experiences which they had in the Welsh Revival of 1904/5 stopped preparing their sermons. They argued that it was no longer necessary, because the Spirit gave them the message. Indeed, I once heard a godly Christian praising a man who was visiting this country at the time to hold meetings, and this was the highest praise he could give him. He said, 'You know it is most wonderful, I have never known anything like it, he never has to prepare an address or a message at all, it is all given to him sometimes as he is walking into the meeting.' Well, that is the kind of thing which one hears said, and these two ministers whom I knew stopped preparing their sermons, because they said, 'We read in Scripture: "Open thy mouth wide, and I will fill it" (Ps 81:10), and doesn't the Scripture say: "Take no thought beforehand what ye shall speak. . . . but whatsoever shall be given you in that hour, that speak ye" (Mk 13:11)?'

The only answer to that is that Scripture must always be taken in its context, and 'Open thy mouth wide and I will fill it' is in a psalm which has nothing to do at all with preaching, but rather it has to do with eating and with food. With regard to the other quotation, it is what the disciples are told to do when they are on trial in court, suddenly arrested and apprehended, and again has nothing to do with preaching and teaching.

In other words, this is not the way to use Scripture. Notice, too, and this to me is most important, that the two ministers, who stopped preparing their messages and would go into the pulpit waiting to receive the message, were godly, honest and sincere men; but I need not tell you that their ministry was completely ruined and their churches disappeared almost under their very hands.

Also, of course, the whole thing is so contrary to the teaching of Scripture itself, which is given in order that it might be expounded. That is why it was written and why there were teachers in the early church, who gave instruction in the Scriptures, who were set aside in order to do so, and who were said to be worthy of double honour.

And as you come down the running centuries, you find that when men had been baptized with the Spirit—men such as Whitefield, Wesley, Moody, Finney [see *Joy Unspeakable*—ed.]—they all expounded the Scriptures, they studied them, they prepared their messages from them and then relied upon the Spirit to give power to it and to apply it to the hearers.

Let me give you a final piece of advice under this general heading. Anything that is merely spectacular should always be regarded with suspicion, or anything that we perceive with our minds and reasons to be foolish should always be under suspicion. In other words, let us always be on the look-out for fanaticism, the hall-mark of which is that it not only overstretches itself but always introduces the element of the ridiculous. Oh how difficult these matters can be!

I am going to give you two examples of this, not to amuse you, for again I am going to refer to two godly men who suffered very much for their faith, and whom I know are now in the glory everlasting. I did not know the first man very well but I knew people who did. This man thought that he was being led of the Spirit to have all his teeth extracted so that a new set might grow. This would be a great and glorious testimony to the work and the power of the Spirit. He said he had been given an assurance about this, it was going to happen, and he actually had his teeth extracted.

I say that this comes under the heading of fanaticism because that man was expecting a new act of creation. You do not get that in the miracles of the Bible. You get healing and restoration but you do not get a new creation. I have heard of people who have prayed for a man who has lost a limb for a new limb to grow; it has never happened. That involves creation. But this is where the counterfeit comes in.

Let me tell you about the second man whom I knew very well indeed. Again he was a minister who was greatly and marvellously used of God in the Welsh Revival of 1904/5, and who was given intimations by the Spirit in a most astonishing manner. He lived at a place about four miles from the sea and one day he announced that it had been revealed to him by the Spirit that he would be enabled to walk on the sea. So he actually went down to the shore in an attempt to do so, which of course ended in nothing but complete failure. And that man, godly saint as he was, was very often depressed and unhappy. Why? Because an evil spirit had, I think, come in and tried to counterfeit and had pressed him too far; this would have been a mere spectacle, with no spiritual benefit.

You remember the kind of thing that the devil suggested to our Lord in the three famous temptations; that he should set himself up on the pinnacle of the temple, and throw himself down, and so on. Now that was just a spectacle and you will find in the history of these matters that the devil often overreaches himself just in that way, by trying to persuade good Christian people to do something that has no value, that is merely spectacular. That is always indicative of a tendency to fanaticism. Indeed the main tendency of the other powers is to press us too far and to urge us in the direction of credulity and an uncritical attitude until the whole thing becomes ridiculous and indeed at times even tragic. And, of course, that is what the devil is ultimately concerned about, that the work of the Spirit and the work of the Lord, shall be brought into ridicule and into contempt.

Well, there we are—we have begun to consider how we carry out the injunction of the Scriptures to 'test the spirits', 'to prove all things' and 'to hold fast that which is good and that which is true'. May God therefore keep us all humble, and guard some against quenching the Spirit. It is a terrible sin to quench the Spirit. And may he guard others from abandoning the gifts which God has given them of reason and understanding, from abandoning even the Scriptures and exposing themselves to the errors, the dangers and the tragedies of fanaticism.

Chapter 5

Safeguards against Error

There are still certain other matters, it seems to me, under this general heading of proving spirits, where great caution is needed. The New Testament exhorts us to be cautious, to prove and to test, not to believe everything that we hear or see. Nothing is more vital than that we should realize that we are in a spiritual realm and that there are principalities and powers and spiritual wickedness even in heavenly places with which we have to contend. The devil himself can transform himself even into an angel of light and deceive almost the very elect themselves if it were possible. Therefore we need great caution. Scripture exhorts us to it, history proves the necessity of it.

The first area where Scripture and church history show the need for extreme caution and wariness is the prophesying of future events. Now I have already partly dealt with this earlier when we considered the tendency to fix the exact date of our Lord's second coming and things like that. That has always been a trap which has been set by the devil, and it is really sad and pathetic to notice how good people have been caught in that way in spite of the exhortation of the Scriptures not to be concerned about the times and the seasons. The devil knows us so well and he knows our curiosity—one of the most prominent characteristics of all of us—how we want to 'know' these things even though we are not meant to know them. The date and time is known only to God.

But this propensity is not confined to our Lord's second coming. You will always find in the history of these aberrations from the New Testament pattern that other particular events have often been prophesied, or a statement made that something particular was going to happen on such and such a date. Robert Baxter did this on several occasions. But I do not want to stay with this. All we need say about it—and we must keep the balance—is that the foretelling of the future is possible, for the Holy Spirit can enable a man to do this . In the annals of some great Scots worthies you will find this very thing. John Welsh and others were enabled to predict accurately certain events which subsequently took place. We must not rule this out, it is always possible. As God gave the gift of prophecy to the prophets in the Old Testament, there is always this possibility which we must not exclude.

All I am saying is that we must be very careful because this is a rare phenomenon. It does occur, but it is a rare phenomenon, so that when you find people doing it freely and without any hesitation you should always be extremely cautious. The ultimate test of the prophet is the one taught us in the Old Testament itself: Does what he has prophesied actually come to pass or not? In the Old Testament, you remember, there was that great struggle going on almost constantly between the true and the false prophets, and both were making prophecies. So the teaching is that, ultimately, you test the truth of the prophet and his claims by that test. You have to wait. If what he says does not happen, then you know he is not a true prophet, and that it is not a word from God.

So when people confidently prophesy that this and that is going to happen on such and such a date and it does not happen, you are made to think. It was largely through this that Robert Baxter eventually came to find that the spirit which was in him, which he had hitherto thought was the Holy Spirit, was clearly not. When a prophecy is given by the Holy Spirit, it does come to pass—it is infallible. So failure is clearly indicative of the fact that it is another spirit.

It would be easy to enlarge on these things, but I must not do so. There is much interest at the present time in what is called extra-sensory perception, an odd ability that some people seem to possess to foretell the future up to a point. Now this should make us see the need of being cautious here. We must realize that in the light of all these things we must be careful lest we too readily ascribe or attribute to the Holy Spirit something which really does not come from him.

Another point where very great caution is needed is the question of 'personal leadings'. Here again is a most extraordinary subject, and indeed a very fascinating one, and, from many angles, a most glorious one. There is no question but that God's people can look for and expect 'leadings', 'guidance', 'indications of what they are meant to do'. There are many examples of this in the Scriptures and I take one at random. You remember the story in Acts 8:26ff of how Philip the Evangelist was told by the angel of the Lord, 'Arise, and go toward the south unto the way that goeth down from Jerusalem unto Gaza, which is desert'. Philip went and, of course, found that he had been sent there in order that he might meet the Ethiopian eunuch and preach Christ to him. Read the story again for yourselves.

Now there are leadings such as that. You get a still more specific one at the beginning of Acts 13, where we are told, 'There were in the church that was at Antioch certain prophets and teachers .... As they ministered to the Lord, and fasted, the Holy Ghost said, Separate me Barnabas and Saul for the work whereunto I have called them.' 'The Holy Ghost said'! They knew that it was the Holy Spirit speaking and they acted upon his instructions. Saul and Barnabas were obedient, because they realized it was the leading of the Spirit.

Again if you read the history of the saints, God's people, throughout the centuries and especially the history of revivals, you will find that this is something which is perfectly clear and definite—men have been told by the Holy Spirit to do something; they knew it was the Holy Spirit speaking to them, and it transpired that it obviously was his leading. It seems clear to me that if we deny such a possibility we are again guilty of quenching the Spirit.

But once more that is not the only thing we have to consider; there is another side to this. Leadings do and can happen. I am sure that many of you who have ever had a specific leading in this respect will not only always thank God for it but look back with a sense of awe upon it as one of the most wonderful and amazing things that has ever happened to you. But we cannot leave it at that, because it does seem to be quite clear in the Scriptures that even the greatest men of God have not habitually lived in a kind of direct, constant leading of the Spirit.

I am going to give you one example which, it seems to me, puts this matter quite clearly—and that is in the case of the apostle Paul himself. Here is one of the most spiritual men the church has ever known, a man baptized with the Spirit, and that, it seems, many times over; the Spirit came upon him and filled him on special occasions. And yet it is interesting to notice that the Apostle obviously did not live perpetually under immediate and direct leadings and guidance of the Spirit. He used his mind and reason and the powers that God had given him, now enlightened and quickened by the Holy Spirit. Let me give you just one example from Acts 16 which is very important in this connection, especially verses 6 and 7: 'Now when they had gone throughout Phrygia and the region of Galatia, and were forbidden of the Holy Ghost to preach the word in Asia, After they were come to Mysia, they assayed to go into Bithynia: but the Spirit suffered them not.'

The two important phrases, of course, are they 'were forbidden of the Holy Ghost to preach the word in Asia', and again, 'they assayed to go into Bithynia: but the Spirit'—'the Spirit of Christ' as some of the manuscripts have it—'suffered them not'. The only conclusion we can come to from this is that the Apostle had decided to preach in Asia, because it seemed to him the right thing to do. He was determined to do it, and the Holy Spirit had to intervene in a special manner to stop him. That, I say, shows that he did not wait until he had some special leading to go into Asia. He had decided to go there, but it was not the will of the Holy Spirit at that point, and so he was hindered. Then in exactly the same way 'they assayed', they attempted, 'to go into Bithynia', and they were proceeding to do so 'but the Spirit suffered them not'.

Now you can draw many conclusions from that, but to me the main one is that clearly the Apostle did not wait for some special leading, even with this great and all-important work. He used his reason and his understanding to reach a decision and when it was not the will of the Spirit, the Spirit would intervene and restrain him and hold him back.

So I would lay down the principle that if we find people beginning to claim special and immediate guidance over practically everything they do, I think we are entitled to have our suspicions aroused. You will find that it comes into their talk. They say that they have been 'led' to do this or that. I have sometimes heard preachers do this and they obviously regarded it as being a mark of unusual spirituality; they prefaced the giving of the text by saying, 'The word to which the Spirit has led me'. Now one should not say that for this reason—a man who is called to the office of the ministry should always submit and subject himself to God, he should always seek the guidance of God in everything and then use the powers that God has given him. But he will sometimes find that he is hindered, and at other times that he has been given a message directly. Thank God that does happen. But when a man gets into the state and condition in which he always waits for that and will do nothing without it, then I say he is on the verge of fanaticism.

This again can be abundantly illustrated from the history of the church. The Quakers, of course, were particularly noticeable in this respect, putting the emphasis as they did upon the 'inner light'; and, with this emphasis upon immediacy and direct leading and guidance increasingly at the expense of the Scriptures, they clearly became open to this particular attack of the devil. Read the story of the early Quakers—it is something worth reading because they bring out an aspect that tends to be forgotten at the present time. But observe it closely, and even as you read it you will find that there was an increasing tendency in some of them to attribute everything to the guidance of the Spirit. You find it in the life of George Fox himself, a man who certainly had many direct leadings and guidance, but not always, as he himself had to discover.

Another notable instance of this and a somewhat surprising one is no less a person than Oliver Cromwell—surely one of the greatest Englishmen who has ever lived. Now here again was a man who, because he was a spiritual man, was a little bit subject to this tendency. He would sometimes hold up parliament or the army council for a day or two and would not give his answer, or judgement, because he was waiting for a direct leading. Nothing is more interesting in the life of the great Lord Protector than the way in which he sought immediate and direct guidance—the term they used then was 'leading'.

Now the danger always is that once you have any experience of such direct leading, you get into the condition in which you cease to function with your normal faculties because you are always waiting for some immediate guidance.

I use my next illustration with considerable fear and trembling, and yet I feel confident that what I am going to say is right. In the history of the 1904-5 revival in Wales, I always feel that the man who was so signally used of God in that revival, the late Mr Evan Roberts, definitely crossed the particular line that I am trying to draw, and got into a state in which he would do nothing without an immediate direct leading of the Spirit. For instance, he might have been announced to preach in a chapel. The people would be there and even he would be there, but he would sit and not speak a word because he said that the Spirit had not led him to do so even though the meeting had been announced and the fact that he was to be present at it. And thus it became increasingly the case with him that he would not take even some of the smallest decisions without some immediate direct guidance. Eventually, of course, he had a breakdown in health and in his nervous constitution. And that has happened to many others who have gone in this particular direction.

I trust I am making this point clear. God forbid that I should say that we should discount everything that appears to be a personal leading. That is just to quench the Spirit. No, it can happen; but beware lest the devil should come and press you so far in that direction that you ultimately become guilty of fanaticism in such a way that you will not do anything without a leading of the Spirit, or regard everything that comes to you as an idea as of necessity being the leading of the Spirit. There are many things attributed to the Holy Spirit which should not be so attributed.

Let me end this subject by telling you the famous story of Charles Haddon Spurgeon which, because it is Spurgeon, has its amusing side. I do not give it to entertain you, however, but to show you a principle enunciated by that great preacher. It is about a man who came to him one day telling him that the Spirit had told him that he (this man) was to preach in Spurgeon's Tabernacle on the following Thursday night. Mr Spurgeon simply replied: 'Well, it seems very odd to me, the Spirit has not told me that.' And so the man did not preach in Spurgeon's Tabernacle. This principle is a very sane one.This is where reason and common sense come in. If the Holy Spirit had meant that man to preach in Spurgeon's Tabernacle, he would also have told Mr Spurgeon, because it was Mr Spurgeon who habitually preached there and who had been announced to preach that evening.

In other words, quench not the Spirit, but prove all things. Do not assume that everything that appears to be a leading of the Spirit *is* a leading of the Spirit. There are ways and means whereby these things can be tested. And there is nothing more dangerous for godly, innocent people, who always want the best, to believe such a man and to accept everything that he says as being of the Holy Spirit because he claims that it is.

We are not, I think, far from the truth if we put it like this: that normally guidance is given to us through the general teaching of the Scriptures and through our own faculties and powers. If we are Christians, the Holy Spirit is in us and he affects, influences and heightens all our faculties. That, plus the teaching of the Scripture, is the normal way of guidance. Anything beyond that by way of direct leading is exceptional and, indeed, there is good scriptural ground, as

I think I have shown you, for saying that the exercise of this direct leading is often as negative and restraining as it is positive and indicative.

This is not an easy subject which is why all this attention to it is so necessary. And as you find people claiming this kind of thing more and more, you have to be cautious with regard to them and, as brethren, you must warn them to be equally cautious also. Any increasing tendency to attribute everything to the Spirit, or this perpetual direct leading, is something that we should always carefully examine.

I go on now to the next principle, which follows on from the last. Anything which makes self prominent or great should always be regarded with the greatest possible suspicion. It is not surprising and yet how difficult it is. A man in the Spirit, anxious for the glory of God and of our Lord, finds that the devil comes to him and tells him, 'Now you are the one who is going to do this for God.' And his mind is chiefly on the glory of the Lord and so he does not see the subtlety of the devil's temptation which is really to put him in a position of prominence.

The history of the church is strewn with tragedies in this respect. Some of the great heretics started by being most godly and great men, but this subtle tendency came in and pride with it. The apostle Paul is constantly warning the early churches against this; for example, in 2 Corinthians 11: 'Would to God ye could bear with me a little in my folly: and indeed bear with me. For I am jealous over you with godly jealousy: for I have espoused you to one husband, that I may present you as a chaste virgin to Christ. But I fear, lest by any means, as the serpent beguiled Eve through his subtilty, so your minds should be corrupted from the simplicity that is in Christ.' That is it! And what Satan played on with Eve and Adam was their pride, of course; pride was the cause of the fall of the devil himself, and the devil always uses this as one of his greatest weapons.

Now this is obvious, but it is tragic to notice how slow people are to see it. And when you yourself are the victim, it is especially difficult to do so. But there are such extraordinary cases in history that the thing should be quite clear to us. One of the early Quakers, called James Naylor, a true man of God, was so pressed by the devil on this point that eventually he was to be found riding a horse into the City of Bristol claiming that he was the Messiah, with a crowd of innocent women and children surrounding him and acclaiming him—a kind of imitation of our Lord's triumphant riding into Jerusalem. Poor Naylor, he was completely led astray at this point. Quite innocently, there is no question. He did not see that it was all self and magnifying Naylor.

And, again, the same thing can be seen very clearly in the story of Robert Baxter, who, poor man, thought that he was to be the messenger of God sent to address the whole country about its future: the message was to be given directly to him. Everything was making Robert Baxter great. But at last, as I have told you, he awakened to a realization of what was happening to him.

Let us now consider the fourth danger point in these matters. This happens when the physical element in connection with the experience is unusually prominent. Here again is a subject that I feel very much needs investigation. By this expression 'physical element' I mean an emphasis upon physical sensations. If there is a lot of talk about the physical aspect of the experience or excitement about it, we should always be extremely suspicious. For example, you get some people describing how they received the baptism of the Spirit in terms of an electric current passing through them, or a great sensation of heat, or seeing a ball of light, or some vision, or something like that.

This kind of thing comes into the question of healing too.

Once again, of course, we must remember that the evil spirits can also heal—there is no doubt about that. For every case that you can produce of spiritual healing as the result of the influence of the Holy Spirit, the spiritists, or spiritualists, whichever you like to call them, can produce an equal number of cases. If you go merely in terms of appearances, and show people who have been crippled and who suddenly find that they can stand and walk and jump and dance—well, the spiritists can show you as many cases as you can show them. How then do we tell the difference?

I think it is just at this very point that what I am putting to you becomes important. You will find in the case of the spiritist healings that there is always emphasis on the physical element. People will testify to a feeling of heat as the hand of the healer came upon them, or of a sensation like an electric shock or something like that—the physical is always very prominent.

I put it like this for this reason. I know I must handle this argument carefully because you must never build a case on the argument from silence, but there is nothing corresponding to that in the New Testament. When men and women were baptized in the New Testament era, they testified to their joy and to the love of God shed abroad in their hearts, and this has been the characteristic of God's people throughout the centuries. They do not talk much about their physical sensations but about their Lord and his love for them and their love for him. Likewise, there is nothing in the case of people healed in the New Testament which tells us anything about this sensation of heat or of electric thrill or current or anything like that. It is just not there. And I feel that it is not there because it is something which is unimportant.

But here, you see, the devil once more falls into the same trap. He always overdoes things, making it spectacular—too spectacular—and he calls attention to the physical concomitants. I am not saying the people in the New Testament did not feel anything physically, they may have done. We are not told, that is all. All they knew was that they were healed, they were whole, they were well, and they attributed the praise and the glory unto God. So if you find people always talking about the sensation of heat or what they felt or the thrill, or the light, or the vision, I say that surely in meeting with something so unlike the pattern of Scripture, you are entitled to regard it with great caution, and are indeed not wrong to be suspicious. It is one of the points that differentiates the spurious from the true.

Let us now move on to another consideration—and here again it is a most important and a very difficult one. This is the whole danger connected with the power of suggestion. With all that is being taught at the present time, and all that has really been brought into prominence during the last hundred years, in particular in the realm of psychology, we can see, perhaps with an especial clarity, the need for caution. The Bible is again proved to be a contemporary and up-to-date book. Its writers did not have the scientific knowledge that we have, but they were aware of the facts. The Holy Spirit knows all, and in New Testament language he tells us to beware of some of these most modern things; not in modern terminology, but in words meaning exactly the same thing.

The power of suggestion is a very real and definite thing. It is always one of the dangers with a crowd, or a mob—we speak of mob or mass psychology. Hitler would never have come to power but for this. He may not consciously have realized what was happening but he was certainly illustrating this very point. He had a kind of hypnotic power; clearly he could make suggestions, and by repetition he could get people to accept them. The people addressed were not conscious of what was happening, but it was the power of suggestion. Now this phenomenon can come into the realm of things spiritual and we are but tyros in these matters unless we realize this. Everything that appears to be conversion is not conversion. You will often find people responding to a call forward in a time of excitement or in a highly organized campaign with large numbers. If you ask them afterwards, 'Why did you go forward?', they will often say, 'I don't know'. And that is the truth—they do not know. It was the power of suggestion; seeing others going forward, they felt an impulse to go and to do the same thing.

Now this can be illustrated, as I say, in many realms. In the political realm it can often be seen in meetings, addressed by someone who is anxious to propagate a doctrine. It is one of the things of which we have to be most wary, and is surely one of the things the Apostle has in his mind when he says in 1 Corinthians 2 that he did not preach in Corinth 'with enticing words of man's wisdom, but in demonstration of the Spirit and of power'. It is because one realizes these dangers that one should avoid them. Far from using psychological techniques and so on, you should avoid them. We all know and have read about these things. You dim the lights and perhaps put a cross, one red cross only, above the pulpit light, and tremendous things can be done. We are all gullible, all liable to these things. And, again, the history of the church tells us a great deal about this—how men, unscrupulous men sometimes, for very mercenary reasons, have used and employed all these things in order to serve their own unworthy purposes.

But what I am anxious to deal with is one particular aspect of this matter that has had a certain amount of prominence recently. It is the phenomenon of speaking with tongues, and one cannot help noticing that this only tends to appear when it is talked or preached about, or when it is suggested in some shape or form. There is a most interesting piece of evidence on this very matter. Some of you may remember a book published several years back called *This is That*. It was an account of the remarkable revival that broke out in the Congo. (Incidentally one cannot but feel that God blessed those people at that time in that way because of what happened to them afterwards. Revivals often come like that to prepare people. It was given in Korea in exactly the same way.) This book tells how this great revival broke out, but there was no manifestation of speaking in tongues except in stations where the subject had already been mentioned and dealt with. In stations where the people had never heard about speaking in tongues, there was no speaking in tongues. This fact was confirmed to me by one of the men most involved in the revival, Mr Ivor Davies. He confirmed that tongues only appeared where they were spoken about.

Surely our suspicions should already be aroused. Or put it another way. If we find that people tend to speak in tongues only as the result of contact with a particular person, preacher or teacher, our suspicions should once more be aroused, because you again have this possibility of suggestion and hypnotic power.

You may be thinking, 'Why do you say this?' I do so because as you read the book of Acts you find that the apostles had this gift of laying their hands upon others who received the Holy Spirit and spoke in tongues, but it is something that seems to have been confined almost entirely to the apostles. I have not forgotten the one exception—Ananias, who was sent, you remember, to the apostle Paul to lay his hands upon him 'that [he] might receive [his] sight and be filled with the Holy Ghost' (Acts 9:17). But that seems to me to confirm the point that this was a gift that was confined to the apostles. Ananias was given a special commission. He was particularly commanded to do what he did, and he obeyed. So that this very exception tends to prove the rule.

Here is a point, I think, that is really beyond any discussion. Let me put it like this to you. If—and it is indeed the teaching of 1 Corinthians 12 that this is the case—if the gift of speaking in tongues is something that is given by the Holy Spirit himself in his sovereignty and in his Lordship, if he is the giver, then he can give it whenever he likes, and he can withhold it whenever he likes. And when it does happen, what will be prominent and evident is not that some particular 'person' has suggested it or taught it, but that it is in truth the gift of the Spirit.

Now why was it that this only happened in the Congo where it had been spoken about, if it is the gift of the Spirit? Why was it confined only to that one particular station and area, if it is all in the sovereignty and the gift and the power of the Spirit?

The answer to that question is perfectly clear to me and I would put it in this form—that if you find this particular phenomenon only occurring as the result of some suggestion or teaching or as the result of the activities of certain particular individuals, then you are fully entitled to be cautious and even suspicious. It is in the sovereignty of the Spirit and he can give and withhold as he pleases. But obviously, if the suggestion is made that all who have the baptism of the Spirit must speak in tongues and this is repeated and repeated, it is not surprising that people begin to speak in tongues. But the question then arises as to what they are doing. That is a question which we shall have to go into later, but all I am concerned about at the moment is that we should never forget the power of suggestion.

What strange creatures we are! It is not even a matter of intellect. You will find that if highly intellectual people get into a spirit of fear they can become very gullible and can therefore mislead many others. We are all subject to these things. But the Scriptures tell us to be careful, to prove, to test, to examine, not to believe every spirit, to remember that there is a power that can counterfeit in a most subtle and brilliant manner so as almost even to deceive the very elect themselves.

I have finished now my list of the particular danger points which I feel we should always keep in the forefront of our minds. The next step is to examine the direct scriptural teaching on this matter. I thank God we are not left in any doubt! There are certain tests which are taught here very plainly and very clearly—specific and explicit tests. I have not dealt with them so far, for we have been considering the 'implicit' tests. We have found in the Scriptures warnings of this great need for caution. We found them there with the use of our mind and reason, and we find them illustrated in the history of the church and the history of particular persons. Oh may God give us balance and wisdom and sanity with respect to these matters!

Let me say again, 'Quench not the Spirit.' To dismiss everything out of hand is not to exercise discrimination; it is to quench the Spirit. If you come to an end of this particular study saying, 'I am not going to touch it. I am not interested in any of it. I am just going on living my Christian life', my dear friend you are quenching the Spirit, and it is a terrible thing to do. No, we must follow the Scriptures. These things are possible and we must always be open. But we must not believe every spirit but 'try the spirits whether they be of God'. Let us thank God for the Scriptures and the illustrations we find in them; let us thank God for the history of the church preserved for us by godly men; let us pay heed to the warnings; and as we see the dangers on the two sides, let us with great humility hold to that simplicity which is in Christ. That, as I hope to show you, is indeed the ultimate test in all these matters.

Chapter 6

Jesus Is Lord

Perhaps it would be good, at this point, to recapitulate on what we have been considering so far. We have seen that it is very important that we should test everything that purports or presents itself to us as being gifts or manifestations of the Spirit. The Scriptures themselves tell us to do that, they urge us to 'jesus is lord'. The Christian is not just some credulous person who believes everything he is told; he is meant to test and to examine. The Scriptures tell us why we must do that: because certain false evil spirits are abroad. That is the great theme of the Bible. In a sense the Bible is a record of the great conflict between God and the devil worked out in various ways. Well, here is this conflict in the very centre and heart of the New Testament. The early church was immediately confronted by this great problem. The devil always tries to ruin the work of God. He ruined the first creation and he tries to do the same with the new creation, so that all who become Christians are immediately special targets of the 'evil one', the 'adversary of the brethren'.

The devil does this work of his in many ways, and one way is to confuse the children of God. He does that by counterfeiting as best he can the manifestations of the work of the

Holy Spirit in the believer, and that is why we are told so constantly to 'prove' and to 'try' and to 'test' the spirits. And we have seen that the way to do that is to use our reason and understanding. They have been given to us by God, and the Holy Spirit enlightens and sharpens them, so that the Christian is to be a highly intelligent person. He is not just an emotionalist, he does not just 'work himself up' emotionally. He is a man who is to use his mind. The great New Testament epistles tax our minds and our understanding. We are meant to use our minds, enlightened as they are by the Spirit. The natural mind does not help here, for it does not even understand what these things are talking about. But given the enlightenment and the unction and the anointing of the Spirit, we are to use our minds and understanding. And then on top of that we are given the clear instruction of the Scriptures themselves.

Now I have put to you a number of general principles derived from the Scriptures—understanding, reason, plus—and very important, not more important than the others, but very important—the history of the church throughout the centuries. Fortunately, we are not the first people who have been engaged in this battle, and there is nothing which can be of greater help to us, next to the Scriptures, than the history of the church. We can see how men and women like ourselves reacted in the same situation, how they fell to temptations at certain points, and all these things are written for our understanding. So we must use them all together to try to arrive at this position in which we can prove and test the spirits. Nothing is more dangerous than to say 'No, I am not interested in what has happened in the past, I am only interested in direct spiritual experiences, I want nothing else.' I have heard people who say that. They are not interested even in the Scriptures; they get it all directly. And there are others who are not interested in church history.

They are the people who are most likely to end in some sort of a disaster.

Having considered some of these general principles, which seem to me to be quite obvious, and which guide us in this matter of testing, we come now directly to the particular teaching in Scripture itself.

The first test, which we must always employ, is the one suggested to us in 1 Corinthians 12:3: 'Wherefore I give you to understand, that no man speaking by the Spirit of God calleth Jesus accursed: and that no man can say that Jesus is the Lord, but by the Holy Ghost.'

At once we are brought face to face with the supreme test, and it is interesting to note that when the Apostle deals later in that chapter with this question of the gifts, and the confusion that had arisen in Corinth because of their misuse, he puts this test at the very beginning. When you are dealing with spiritual gifts, he says, you must always put this first.

1 John 4, you remember, says precisely the same thing: 'Beloved, believe not every spirit, but try the spirits whether they are of God: because many false prophets are gone out into the world. Hereby know ye the Spirit of God: Every spirit that confesseth that Jesus Christ is come in the flesh is of God: And every spirit that confesseth not that Jesus Christ is come in the flesh is not of God: and this is that spirit of antichrist, whereof ye have heard that it should come; and even now already is it in the world.'

Those two statements confirm, of course, what our Lord himself said, as it is recorded in John 16. You remember how just at the very end of his ministry and before his death upon the cross, our Lord taught the disciples concerning the Holy Spirit and his work. They were crestfallen because he had told them that he was going to leave them, and they wondered what was going to happen to them. The answer was that the Holy Spirit was to come. And our Lord instructed them about him and told them what he was going to do.

The crucial statement is in verse 14: 'He shall glorify me: for he shall receive of mine, and shall shew it unto you.' Now that is absolutely basic. 'He'—the Holy Spirit when he comes—Christ says, 'shall glorify me.' This is the supreme test of anything that claims to be the work of the Holy Spirit. Indeed, our Lord had already said much the same thing earlier on in that same chapter, beginning at verse 7: 'Nevertheless', he tells them, 'I tell you the truth; It is expedient for you that I go away: for if I go not away, the Comforter will not come unto you; but if I depart, I will send him unto you. And when he is come, he will reprove the world of sin, and of righteousness, and of judgment: Of sin'—why?—'because they believe not on me'—always pointing to him—'Of righteousness, because I go to my Father, and ye see me no more; Of judgment, because the prince of this world is judged.' And he judged that enemy by dying upon the cross.

There then we have our Lord himself laying down the great principle that the supreme and outstanding characteristic of the work of the Holy Spirit will always be to glorify him. The Spirit will not speak out of or from himself, or even call attention to himself. He will always—if I may use such an expression—focus a light upon the Son of God.

This is a most wonderful thought. You remember how our Lord himself kept on saying about his own ministry that he had come to glorify the Father. There are many Christian people who forget that. There are many Evangelicals who very rarely speak about the Father, but only about the Son; whereas the Son himself said so often that he had come to glorify the Father and to bring us to him. And in exactly the same way there are people who seem to talk only about the Spirit and forget that the Spirit has come to glorify the Son. This, therefore, is *the* test of all tests which we must apply to anything that claims to be the work of the Holy Spirit of God.

Now what does this mean exactly? What is this test as put by Paul to the Corinthians and by John in his epistle? It means acknowledging the truth about the Lord Jesus Christ and his person. 'Jesus is Lord!' That is the great confession! It was the great confession of the early church. 'Jesus Christ is Lord!' And it was in terms of this test that so many of the early Christians were martyred. They were being asked to say, 'Caesar is Lord', but they would not. No, Jesus is Lord and he alone is 'the Lord'.

To glorify him means that we believe the truth concerning his person, that he is indeed the only begotten Son of God. If a man does not believe in the unique deity of the Lord Jesus Christ, nor in his eternal Sonship; if he does not believe in his co-equality and co-eternity with the Father, nor in the great doctrine of the incarnation, then this man is simply not a Christian and he has not got the Spirit of God in him. He may claim to be a Christian, he may even be a so-called Christian preacher, and have prominence in the church, but if he denies that Jesus is God, he has not the Holy Spirit in him.

This is essential—'that Jesus Christ is come in the flesh' as John puts it in 1 John 4. Notice, too, that the two sides of his nature are prominent—his eternal Godhead and the reality of his human body. There were men appearing in the churches who taught that the incarnation was not really a fact, that Jesus, the 'Lord of Glory', had taken on a kind of phantom body, and that he was not really man. Others were saying that he was *only* man. Both are denounced in the New Testament. So we have to assert, and the Holy Spirit makes us do so, that 'Jesus is Lord', that 'Jesus Christ is truly come in the flesh'.

There is a tradition concerning the apostle John in his old

age that as he was entering a certain bath house, he was told that Celsus, one of these heretics who denied the reality of our Lord's manhood, was there having a bath. The moment John heard this he turned away and would not even be in the same building with such a man. And that is of course right. How much more terrible it is that such men are to be found in the Christian church; men who deny the reality of the incarnation, or who deny one or the other of the two natures in the one person of the Son of God.

And then the Holy Spirit enables one to understand not only the person but also the work of Christ. It is the Holy Spirit alone who can enable one to understand the bread and wine of the communion table and why we observe this sacrament, and what it means. People deny this, they ridicule it or explain it away, calling Christ a pacifist or just a good man. But the Holy Spirit brings a man to see that there on the cross he is bearing our sins and their punishment. 'God was in Christ, reconciling the world unto himself, not imputing their trespasses unto them' (2 Cor 5:19). It is the Spirit alone that can bring a man to see these things, and denial of any one of them means that it is neither Christianity, nor the Christian message.

I want to add another test to this first one. It means not only that you believe these things about the Lord, but that you give the central place to him. That is why I am emphasizing this aspect of the matter, that the Holy Spirit is to glorify him. And it is enlightening to notice that in the remainder of the New Testament following the gospels it is still the Lord Jesus Christ who dominates the situation. There are some people who try to persuade us to call the book of the Acts of the Apostles, the book of the Acts of the Holy Spirit. But that would be quite wrong. Luke himself makes that perfectly clear at the beginning of the book: 'The former treatise have I made, O Theophilus, of all that *Jesus* began both to do and to teach.' It is Jesus who goes on doing it. There you see the great activity of the Spirit. It is the Lord Jesus Christ who stands out, who dominates the scene. Acts is the continuing story of his work. The Spirit leads men to glorify the Lord Jesus Christ.

Thirdly, this term 'Jesus is Lord' means, of course, that we surrender ourselves to him. You may think that when the Apostle says, 'No man can say that Jesus is the Lord, but by the Holy Ghost' what he means is that if a man gets up and says, 'Jesus is Lord', he is automatically a Christian. But it does not mean that. This is a very profound statement. If you said, 'Jesus is the Lord', in the ancient world of the first century, it might very well mean martyrdom for you. If you were a Jew, it would certainly mean that you were ostracized from your family and your name expunged from the family tree. A man who says, 'Jesus is Lord', and means what he says, is one who has surrendered his life to him, who has joined the church, and who is often exposed to persecution and ridicule and misunderstanding. So the confession that 'Jesus is Lord' is not just repeating a phrase; anybody can do that. The empty repetition of a phrase does not mean that a man is guided, led, moved and indwelt by the Holy Spirit. This is the profoundest statement of all. It is the ultimate; not only the acceptance of the faith, but commital of oneself to it, casting all one's hopes and fears and everything upon him, taking up the cross and following him.

Here, then, is the first and the greatest test, one which obviously excludes many things that offer themselves to us and claim to be Christian. It is, therefore, an excluding test, and most valuable in that respect. I mentioned earlier some of the history of the Quakers, and they are particularly interesting in this respect. Having started as fully orthodox Christians, like the other Puritans in the seventeenth century, the Quakers, by putting their emphasis increasingly upon the inner light and discounting the teaching of the word began to go astray in their doctrine. I am not being at all critical of them or unfair to them when I assert that by today the vast majority of them are unitarians.

Now this is no accident, it is the kind of thing that happens. People may come to you, they may give every appearance of being very spiritual, highly moral people, who may do excellent works—they may be the greatest philanthropists in the country—but that is not enough. The question we want to know is this—and here is our most valuable excluding test—what do they say about this Jesus? What is their confession with respect to him? Is he just the great teacher, just the supreme mystic, or is he the Son of God incarnate, who saves by his death upon the cross, by his body being broken and his blood being shed? These are the tests, and if you apply them you will discover the interesting result.

This test does not only apply to the Quakers, but also to many of the cults that are current at the present time, as well as those that have had their day and their vogue in past centuries. You will find that this preliminary test is always of great value. You may get people coming to you and using very wonderful language and professing great idealism. They may talk to you about miracles of healing, wonderful guidance and various other things. It all sounds so Christian, and they seem to be offering most of the things listed in the gifts of the Spirit. But you must not accept all that at face value. It may sound like the Christian position but that is where the subtlety comes in. You have got to 'prove', and to 'test', and the test you apply is this: what do they say about the Lord Jesus Christ? They may well have miracles to offer you, or wonderful experiences to give you; they may be able to put people forward to give their testimony and say, 'I used to be miserable and unhappy, now I am happy all the day and I have got no troubles and problems and all is bright and glorious.' But you listen to them, and listen for one thing only—where does the Lord Jesus Christ come in? And you will generally find that he does not come in at all. If he is mentioned, it seems he is just the first propagator of this particular teaching—Christ, the first Christian Scientist, for instance. He had the right view of life, they say, the true science, philosophy and understanding of life; he is just the first propounder and exemplar of this or that, and no more than that. He is not the Son of God. He is not eternal and he does not save by dying on the cross—there is no atonement.

In other cases, you find he is not mentioned at all. It sounds like the real thing: people feel much better; they have had a wonderful experience or a great deliverance; they have been healed physically. Surely, you say, this is Christianity, the very thing we want; indeed it is so much better than what the churches offer, we do not find these things in the churches. This is real Christianity. Be careful, my friend, be careful! Apply the first great excluding test, what do they say about the Lord? Where does he come in in all their teaching and their scheme? Is he the eternal Son of God? Does he save by shedding his blood? Is he central, is he essential, is he all-important?

But having said all that and emphasized all these things, I have now to say that even that important test is not enough! You notice that I have kept on referring to it as essentially an 'excluding' test, and I have been doing that very deliberately, because it is not enough. You might interpret these statements as meaning that if a man comes and tells me that he believes that Jesus is Lord, then obviously I must accept everything he says and everything he does. You might think that because he says, 'Jesus is Lord', he must be right in every respect. But that does not follow, and this is where this whole necessity for testing becomes so subtle and so delicate.

Now on what grounds do I say that? Well, let me give you my evidence. I am not here to give voice to my own opinions; God knows we all have to be careful; so let us listen to Scripture. Read what our Lord says in Matthew 24:23—'Then if any man shall say unto you, Lo, here is Christ, or there; believe it not. For there shall arise false Christs, and false prophets, and shall shew great signs and wonders; insomuch that, if it were possible, they shall deceive the very elect.' What a statement! False Christs! People will say, 'Here is Christ, or there is Christ.' Do not believe them. Read that passage again. Those are the words of our blessed Lord himself, and he says that this is going to become particularly true towards the 'end of the world', the 'end of this age'.

Look at a comparable statement in 2 Thessalonians 2:8-9—'And then shall that Wicked be revealed, whom the Lord shall consume with the spirit of his mouth, and shall destroy with the brightness of his coming: Even him, whose coming is after the working of Satan with all power and signs and lying wonders.' Exactly the same thing is being prophesied and it is because of these things that we have to exercise such great care.

All these warnings are addressed to the church, not to the world. It means that all these things are going to happen in terms of the Christian message. Look again at 2 Corinthians 11. This was the great problem in Corinth: they got so excited about the different gifts and so on that they were losing their balance, and so Paul has to keep on repeating the warning to them. He begins like this: 'Would to God ye could bear with me a little in my folly: and indeed bear with me. For I am jealous over you with godly jealousy: for I have espoused you to one husband, that I may present you as a chaste virgin to Christ. But I fear, lest by any means, as the serpent beguiled Eve through his subtilty, so your minds should be corrupted from the simplicity that is in Christ (2

Cor 11:1-3). There is the warning. The moment we get away from this central simplicity that is in Christ we are already doing something that is extremely dangerous.

Paul continues with this theme later in the same chapter. He is talking about certain other teachers who were going round the churches as Christian teachers. Now this is so important. They were not going round as people denying the Christian faith, but as Christian preachers, and they were confusing the churches. Paul says of them, 'Such are false apostles, deceitful workers, transforming themselves into the apostles of Christ. And no marvel; for Satan himself is transformed into an angel of light. Therefore it is no great thing if his ministers also be transformed as the ministers of righteousness; whose end shall be according to their works' (verses 13-15). Could anything be plainer? They appear as apostles of Christ, and yet they are false teachers.

So these warnings go on. Another is given to us by our Lord early in his ministry, even in the Sermon on the Mount itself. Matthew 7:21-23 tells us: 'Not every one that saith unto me, Lord, Lord, shall enter into the kingdom of heaven; but he that doeth the will of my Father which is in heaven. Many will say to me in that day, Lord, Lord, have we not prophesied in thy name? and in thy name have cast out devils? and in thy name done many wonderful works?' And he does not deny that they have done them. 'Then will I profess unto them, I never knew you: depart from me, ye that work iniquity.' He does not deny that they have had the power to do the works when they claim that they have done some wonderful thing, and done it in his name.

You see, this is where we have got to be so careful. You may say, 'Oh yes, with regard to the cults it is plain enough. We have applied your test, and as they do not believe about our Lord as we read in the New Testament—indeed many of them do not even mention him—then that is perfectly clear.

But surely when a man comes along and says he has done it in the name of the Lord, he must be right.' No! it does not follow. Read the passage again. Is this point not very plain, my friends? It is not enough that people should 'say' that Jesus is the Lord.

Let me give you further proof of what I am saying, and show you further the importance of applying these tests, because these evil spirits can make most extraordinary statements in order to delude us. Read Mark 3:11—'And unclean spirits, when they saw him, fell down before him, and cried, saying, Thou art the Son of God.' Here are evil spirits falling down before him in the persons of their victims and making the confession, 'Thou art the Son of God.' So it is obviously not sufficient that people should say, 'Jesus is Lord'; evil spirits may say that. Here they were, according to the record, doing that in the very days when our Lord was here in this world. You get the same thing reported in Luke 4:41—'And devils also came out of many, crying out, and saying, Thou art Christ the Son of God. And he rebuking them suffered them not to speak: for they knew that he was Christ.' As James reminds us, 'The devils also believe, and tremble' (Jas 2:19). So the mere statement of an orthodox view does not guarantee that the work that is being performed is of necessity the work of the Holy Spirit.

Let me give you one final example from Acts, which shows how the apostles in turn put this very teaching into practice. It is the famous incident in the ministry of the apostle Paul when he and Silas were at Philippi. In Acts 16:16, we read: 'It came to pass, as we went to prayer, a certain damsel possessed with a spirit of divination met us, which brought her masters much gain by soothsaying: The same followed Paul and us, and cried, saying, These men are the servants of the most high God, which show unto us the way of salvation.' Would you not have expected Paul to have added her immediately to his evangelistic party as just the very thing he needed? Here is a girl obviously possessed with some wonderful powers. She points at them day after day as they go by and continues to make these statements about them. What a wonderful advertising agency, you might have thought, for the preaching of the gospel. No, no! Verse 18 continues: 'And this did she many days. But Paul, being grieved, turned and said to the spirit, I command thee in the name of Jesus Christ to come out of her. And he came out the same hour.'

Now I trust that these pieces of evidence are more than sufficient to convince us that even if the confession is made of the name of Christ, it does not guarantee that everything that is being done is of necessity the work of the Holy Spirit. The Scriptures warn us.

Let us see how history again confirms all this. I could give you many examples. The history of the church is strewn with examples of people who have been misled at this very point. Most of the heretics went astray just here; and most of the aberrant, fanatical movements, which have caused such trouble, went astray in exactly the same way. Let me give you just one example—Robert Baxter. I use him again because I have already mentioned him earlier. The same thing was true, of course, of Edward Irving himself and of all the people who used to worship together. These people were true Christians. You could not wish for a more orthodox Christian than Robert Baxter, whose great desire was to exalt the name of the Lord Jesus Christ. There was no doubt about that. He unquestionably passed the test of 1 Corinthians 12:3 and of 1 John 4:1-3. He did confess that Jesus Christ was come in the flesh. He was very much concerned to do that. And yet, as I have already mentioned, poor Robert Baxter made the terrible discovery that the spirit that was in him, which he had thought was the Holy Spirit, was clearly not the Holy Spirit, and he thanked God for delivering him from a possibly terrible fate.

Here, then, is the very essence of this problem. We cannot rest on that one test, although we are tempted to do so. We all, I suppose, have done this at some time or another. Someone comes along and speaks in a certain way, tells you of a certain experience he has had, or reports to you certain things that have been happening. You have various hesitations, but you say that the man is patently a fine Christian and utterly orthodox in his belief. Because he is genuine, sincere, and all out for the glory of God and of Christ, we feel that what he says must, therefore, be right. So you overrule your desire to test and to prove; in fact you feel it is almost wrong to do so, that you would almost be sinning against the Holy Spirit or guilty of blasphemy even to question and to query such a person. And yet I trust I have demonstrated to you that you must test such a person. 'Believe not every spirit; but test and prove and try the spirits whether they be of God or not.' Some of the most genuine people are the ones who have gone most grievously astray, simply because they have not realized that this one test is not enough. You will find, indeed, in the history of Robert Baxter that when questions did arise in his mind, and especially when his wife expressed her concern about what was happening to him and what he was doing, and reasoned with him out of the Scriptures—the only answer he kept on giving was, 'I don't know, but all I know is that Christ is more real to me and I am more concerned for his glory, and I love him more than I have ever done.' That seemed to answer everything. But it is not enough. We must go on testing and proving and trying the spirits.

What then do we do in the light of all this? Well, thank God that in the New Testament there are still more specific tests, which we must examine. If the Apostle had felt that merely to say that 'Jesus is Lord' was enough, he would never have written the rest of 1 Corinthians 12, or chapters 13 and 14. He would have said, this alone matters. But he knew better and so he had to go on and deal with the subject in detail. And I would like to do that with you.

Let me say again that my reason for doing so is not some theoretical or academic interest. I have but one concern. To me the one thing that should be uppermost in our minds at this moment is the need of the Christian church for a baptism of the Spirit, to lift her out of her formality and lethargy and deadness. Nothing is more urgent than a great revival of religion. You see the moral declension. It is no use just condemning it—I hope to show how futile that is. What is needed is this power of the Holy Spirit upon the word, the authentication of the message, the orthodox message of the Christian church, a sifting of the true from the false, and then for God to come down upon this word of truth. It is the supreme need, and all who are concerned about that are, in my opinion, following directly the leading of the Spirit himself.

But the moment we do that the other spirit will come in. He will try to spoil it by counterfeiting it or pressing us too far along certain lines; he will get people to confuse the baptism of the Spirit with the occasional gifts of the Spirit, and people will reject both together, and the great need of revival will be forgotten. That is why I am dealing with this matter and it has got to be done in detail. The apostle Paul was a very busy man, a traveller and an evangelist, who did not have time just to sit down in a study and write letters to churches. No, he never wrote a letter unless he had to do so, and he was concerned and troubled about the church at Corinth. He says he was 'jealous over them with a godly jealousy'. He wanted to save them from themselves and their own errors, to save the reputation of the church because she was the church of Christ, of God, and he wanted to save the reputation, as it were, of God the Father, the Son and the Holy Spirit. So we too must be imbued with the same desire.

Let me, then, just introduce this subject to you now, and then we will go on to look at it and to consider it in detail. The great trouble I often find with 1 Corinthians 12, 13 and 14 is that people become so interested in the details over particular gifts that they miss the whole message of these three chapters. Nowhere is the danger of missing the wood for the trees greater than just at this point. In other words, the first thing you must do is to ask a question. Why did the Apostle write this section? What is his ultimate object? What is he really trying to do? Is he trying to tell us about tongues or about healings? No, he is not; he assumes these things. What he is concerned about is that we should get all these things into the right perspective and balance. He did not write these chapters in order to give a disquisition on the gifts of the Spirit. That is not his object at all! There was trouble and confusion and even division in the church at Corinth over these matters, and the Apostle's one object is to straighten that out and to put it right.

So we must not be over-concerned about the details. We must grasp first and foremost the overriding principle, the grand objective. Here you are, he seems to be saying, dividing up and vying with one another. Listen: 'I give you to understand that no man speaking by the Spirit of God calleth Jesus accursed: and that no man can say that Jesus is the Lord, but by the Holy Ghost.' Have you forgotten about Jesus? *That* is what he is really saying. And then, of course, he works it out in terms of his analogy of the body and so on, showing that a true balance with regard to these things has an essential unity, which all focuses in the person of the Lord Jesus Christ.

Now that is the great leading principle which we must have in mind as we follow the Apostle as he works it out in detail. I am not going to do anything but expound to you in a very general way the teaching of these three chapters. It is no part of my object—indeed, it is unnecessary that we should take these nine gifts in detail and say what each one means. I think if we do that we are likely to fall into the very error against which the Apostle is trying to safeguard us. The central principle is to have a balanced and true view of the purpose and place of all these things in the life of those who truly believe that Jesus is the Lord. And as we follow the teaching, I think we shall be saved from many of the dangers that beset us, and have beset the church at many different times. Notice the last verse of chapter 14, just to finish with this general principle. Here is the object: 'Let all things be done decently and in order.' Paul writes these three chapters because the church at Corinth had become 'indecent and disorderly' in a spiritual sense. This is the error he is seeking to redress.

Chapter 7

Seeking the Gifts

In our consideration of this subject of the baptism with the Holy Spirit we have come to the point where we are considering the matter of the spiritual gifts. The baptism with the Holy Spirit, as we have seen, is essentially designed for witness. Our Lord told the disciples, 'Tarry ye in the city of Jerusalem until ye be endued with power from on high' (Lk 24:49), and then he tells them that they would be 'witnesses unto him'. As they were they were not yet fit to be witnesses. Let us never forget that these words were uttered to the disciples who had been with our Lord during the three years of his ministry. They had heard his sermons, they had seen his miracles, they had seen him crucified on the cross, they had seen him dead and buried, and they had seen him after he had risen literally in the body from the grave. These were the men who had been with him in the upper room at Jerusalem after his resurrection and to whom he had expounded the Scriptures, and yet it is to these men he says that they must tarry at Jerusalem until they are endued with power from on high. The special purpose, the specific purpose of the baptism with the Holy Spirit is to enable us to witness, to bear testimony, and one of the ways in which that happens is through the giving of spiritual gifts. That is why we must consider this subject in dealing with the general doctrine of the baptism with the Holy Spirit.

We have already seen that it is possible for one to be baptized with the Holy Spirit without having some of these special gifts. That is made clear in this passage in 1 Corinthians 12-14 and it is made equally clear in the long history of the Christian church. There have been men raised up of God, baptized with the Spirit—and I am thinking of men such as Whitefield and the Wesley brothers, Finney and D.L. Moody and others—clearly and patently baptized with the Holy Spirit as a separate experience, but they never spoke in tongues and they did not work miracles. It is vital that we should keep these things distinct and clear in our minds.

Now that does not mean to say that there are to be no manifestations of gifts at the present time. We have seen that we must be open to this. We disagree with those who say that these things were confined to the apostolic period; we disagree equally with those who say that all these things should always be manifest in the church. We say that it is a matter for the sovereignty of the Spirit, and clearly throughout the centuries in revival in various times in the church the Spirit has manifested this sovereignty. He has given power of utterance, power of speech, power of preaching oftentimes without some of these particular gifts.

However, it is vital that we should consider these things because at any time, at any moment, the Spirit in his sovereignty may decide to give these gifts again. That is why we should be familiar with the teaching for we have seen that there is great cause for spiritual caution in these matters. We are exhorted to test and to prove the spirits, and that is what we are now trying to do. We see that we do so by the employment of our reason and understanding, particularly with regard to the Scriptures, and that the Holy Spirit will enlighten our minds as we read them. And we have seen so far that the first and the greatest test of all is the place given to our blessed Lord.

But we have also seen that even that is not enough in and of itself. It excludes a lot, but it is not enough to exclude various other counterfeits that may be worked by the devil. So we come now to consider the teaching of these three great chapters, 1 Corinthians 12, 13 and 14. Now Paul, you remember, makes it particularly clear that he was not writing to the Corinthians just for the pleasure of it, but for one reason only, and that was because it had become essential. The church had become divided up into groups and sects and divisions. They were a carnally minded church, divided up amongst themselves even with regard to their teachers and preachers—I am of Paul, I am of Apollos, I am of Cephas—divided again about whether they should eat meat offered to idols or not. These things had become matters of division and they were particularly in trouble over this question of spiritual gifts, which is why the Apostle writes to them. If they had not abused these gifts, he probably would never have written about this matter; but they had, and so Paul's whole object in this passage is to correct this abuse. Confusion had arisen among the Christians in Corinth owing to the fact that they were suffering from a lack of proportion in their understanding of these spiritual gifts.

The Apostle writes to them almost with a sense of astonishment. He tells them that they should be children in malice, but to be men in understanding. 'Brethren, be not children in understanding: howbeit in malice be ye children, but in understanding be men' (1 Cor 14:20). They were behaving like children, and he writes to them in order to give them a right sense of proportion with regard to these matters.

So, then, what is Paul's teaching? I have tried to classify it by picking out the principles. I am not concerned to go into the details of the particular gifts. That is a right thing to do, but it is not really essential for the present purpose, because what is true of any one gift is true of all the gifts, since they are all given by the one and the selfsame Spirit, as he keeps on emphasizing—indeed that is his main point, as we shall see. The first and foremost principle concerns the place and the purpose of these gifts in the life of the individual Christian and in the life of the church. Here the Apostle's teaching is surely quite plain, namely that they must never be regarded as ends in themselves—never! That is the danger that people regard these gifts as ends in themselves and forget their whole object and purpose. The moment we do that, we have got them out of proportion. They must be considered in their setting, in their object, and in their whole purpose, and that is what the Apostle proceeds to show these people.

In other words, the gifts must never be put in the centre. They were becoming central in Corinth, occupying the very centre of the stage as it were, and that is why the Apostle has to rebuke the Corinthian church. He says, You have got this out of proportion, they are not meant to be central. In other words, we must never be constantly talking about the gifts. There is a place for them, but not in the centre of our conversation, or our preaching and teaching.

Now this is what is so interesting. Take the New Testament itself and you cannot but see that what dominates the New Testament in the central position is the Lord Jesus Christ himself, and everything points to him. There are many other things that are incidental, including this question of the gifts. But it is not the gifts that are central to the New Testament; it is the Lord.

Again you will find that in the great periods of reformation and revival in the church, when remarkable things have happened and phenomena have been evident, it is not the wonders that have been at the centre, but the Lord himself.

These things have simply pointed to him. So that the moment we find ourselves constantly talking about gifts, any one of them or all of them together, and putting them in the centre of our teaching and preaching, we have already lost the balance and proportion. They are never meant to occupy the centre of the stage. It is still worse, of course, when they become the cause of division or when they divide a church up into sects as they had done at Corinth. It is because of this that Paul writes his letters and he reprimands them. They are very wrong in doing this. So it seems to me that to form movements with respect to the gifts of the Spirit is utterly unscriptural.

But let us be fair in this matter. This does not only apply to spiritual gifts. The way in which people have formed movements with respect to particular matters never ceases to amaze me. For instance, I cannot see in the New Testament itself any possible justification for a movement in connection with holiness. I cannot see any justification for a movement just to teach prophetic teaching or concerning the second advent of our Lord. We should not form movements with regard to particular aspects of the faith or of doctrine. No; the moment you do so you lose your balance. All these things should always be taken together; in the same way there must be no movement in connection with the gifts of the Spirit. Why? Because these are to be manifested in the church, and the church is a whole and her doctrine is a whole. You do not 'specialize' on doctrines in the Christian life.

This is something, of course, which one could illustrate from many other realms. Over-specialization is always a danger. For what it is worth it seems to me that this is what is happening in modern medicine, and it is a very dangerous thing. You get men who specialize exclusively on the chest, while others only know about abdominal conditions, which is very dangerous because you may have a disease in your chest, but your pain may well be in your abdominal area. They are parts of a body and you should not divide the body up like that. And it is exactly the same with the various aspects of Christian teaching or of the various manifestations of the life and the power of the Holy Spirit in man. The moment these things are isolated and are put in a special position, with all the attention focused on them, you have already lost your New Testament balance and sense of proportion. So I say that it is surely evident that when an individual or a number of individuals are always talking about gifts, and never talking about anything else, and while they are always preaching and teaching this, they have already gone into the Corinthian position.

That does not mean to say that the gifts themselves are wrong, but it does mean that this attitude towards them is wrong and that these people are already in a position which is contrary to the teaching of Scripture. They are too excited about them. They were very excited in Corinth about these things. As you read these chapters you can feel the tension and the excitement. The whole church was in a condition in which the Apostle had to reprimand them and write the great thirteenth chapter on love in order to bring them back to a right sense of balance with regard to these matters.

Then another obvious thing about them was that they were lacking in a sense of discipline with respect to the gifts, and they were guilty of a certain amount of disorder and, indeed, of causing a riot. Paul emphasizes, 'Let all things be done decently, and in order.' They were so undisciplined that he has to say to them: 'If therefore the whole church be come together into one place, and all speak with tongues, and there come in those that are unlearned, or unbelievers, will they not say that ye are mad?' (1 Cor 14:23). When the church gives the impression to the outsider that she consists of a number of maniacs, she is doing the exact opposite of what our Lord intended her to do. There was great disorder here, simply because they were not viewing these gifts in the right way; gifts had become everything and they all wanted to show that they had got the gifts, and they were all doing it at the same time. And so a stranger coming in and hearing all these people speaking in tongues at the same time, would say, 'They are mad!'

Another terrible thing that had arisen was that a spirit of competition had come in with respect to the gifts. That is the burden of the middle section of the twelfth chapter. Paul writes, 'The body is not one member, but many. If the foot shall say, Because I am not the hand, I am not the body; is it therefore not of the body?' (verse 14). You see these gifts differ. Paul lists nine different gifts, some of which are more spectacular than others. Because they had got the whole subject out of proportion, they became jealous of one another, and the men with the greater gifts tended to despise the others, so that the whole church was in a state of turmoil. As well as showing an utter lack of discipline, the Corinthians were literally filled with envy of one another. The whole condition of the church was a most unhappy and a most unfortunate one.

This sense of competition had led to the tendency to 'display' the gifts. The Christian life is a very wonderful life, it is a new life; but we are still in the body, and not yet made perfect. There are infirmities that remain, and there is the devil, the adversary, who is always ready to upset the work of God. When these gifts are given, the devil comes in and gets us to view them in the wrong way, and so we begin to display ourselves and show off the gift.

I need not expand on these things, they are always important. They are important, for example, in prayer meetings, as I have often had to point out. The ideal prayer meeting is one in which almost everybody present takes part, but sometimes some people pray at such length that there is no time for anybody else. But Paul teaches here that we should think of one another, and not be making a display. They were guilty of doing that in Corinth and it is always one of the dangers that tends to creep in.

Then, finally, under this heading, the thing that the Apostle emphasizes is the importance of putting the gifts into the right order. There is no doubt at all that the main trouble in Corinth was that the gift of tongues was being given too much prominence. That is the main thrust of the three chapters. Paul always puts it last on the list.

Now let us be clear about this. Paul says quite specifically 'prohibit not to speak in tongues'. We must not do that. But it is equally clear that he says, Do not put it first, do not monopolize the whole of the life of the church in speaking in tongues as that is not its place. He says, 'Covet earnestly the best gifts'; adding later on in chapter 14, 'Follow after charity, and desire spiritual gifts, but rather that ye may prophesy.' To show the importance of prophecy over and against tongues, he gives us this teaching with regard to the respective merits of prophesying and speaking in tongues. Indeed, the whole of that fourteenth chapter is designed to show that tongues must never be the one thing to be talked about; it must not be the one thing that everybody covets nor must it monopolize all the attention—that is what he condemns. The gifts must be put in the right order. The gift of tongues is a very spectacular and exciting one, and that is exactly where the devil sees his opportunity. He gets people to lose their sense of balance and proportion, so that this becomes the centre. It should not be; it is always put last in the list, and seems to be the least of the gifts. It is a spiritual gift; 'I would that ye all spake with tongues', says Paul. Obviously they did not all do so, otherwise he would not say that. He says that he himself speaks in tongues, and thanks God for it, but he keeps it in order and in its right place. Paul says, 'In the church I had rather speak five words with my understanding.... than ten thousand words in an unknown tongue.'

So we see how these things can be abused because people forget the place and the purpose and the object of all these gifts, which is to glorify the Lord. That is the thing that people will keep on forgetting. They stop at the gifts themselves. 'Isn't it wonderful,' they say, 'isn't it marvellous.' But where is the Lord, my friend, where is he? All these things are meant to glorify the Lord! How is it that we can so often forget the pattern and the example which is set for us by the apostles themselves?

Look at that great incident in Acts 3 when Peter and John went up to the temple at the hour of prayer. They saw the lame man laid daily at the Beautiful gate and were enabled to heal him. Here was a man who had never walked in his life and Peter said to him, 'Silver and gold have I none; but such as I have give I thee: In the name of Jesus Christ of Nazareth rise up and walk.' In the actual performance of the miracle Peter is careful to put the Lord at the very centre. He had been given this gift, this is the gift of miracles being exercised. But notice the way in which the Apostle performs the miracle.

It becomes still more interesting when Peter addresses the crowd that had gathered together. They were filled with wonder and amazement, 'And when Peter saw it, he answered unto the people, Ye men of Israel, why marvel ye at this? or why look ye so earnestly on us, as though by our own power or holiness we had made this man to walk?' He will not let himself be placed in the centre, nor have attention focused on himself. He says, 'The God of Abraham, and of Isaac, and of Jacob, the God of our fathers, hath glorified his Son Jesus; whom ye delivered up, and denied him in the presence of Pilate, when he was determined to let him go . . . . His name through faith in his name hath made this man strong, whom ye see and know: yea, the faith which is by him hath given him this perfect soundness in the presence of you all.' Peter goes on preaching Jesus Christ. He does not give them an address on gifts, he manifests the gift. The purpose of the gift is to call attention to the Lord. You do not stop with the gifts, and attention should not be focused on them. You should not be always preaching and teaching about the gifts. No, you are to preach Christ! You are to preach what he does, how he sends the Spirit, and how the Spirit in turn may or may not give the gifts.

You do not found a movement on gifts, because if you do you will find that you are saying very little about the Lord. And any teaching or preaching which does not keep the Lord central and vital and overruling everything is already wrong teaching. That kind of teaching always leads to trouble and eventually to disaster. Let us not forget that this is what happened to the Irvingite movement. What a contrast all this is to the mighty preaching that has always characterized the great revivals in the history of the church. They preached Jesus Christ as Saviour and as Lord. He was the centre of all the preaching. This emphasis is even reflected in the hymns that we have in our hymn books, the great hymns. They are all focused on him. And once we cease to realize that the object of all the gifts is to glorify him—the moment we forget that, we have already gone wrong.

The second object of the gifts is evangelistic. The Apostle makes this quite plain, for instance, with regard to this gift of tongues, 'Wherefore tongues are for a sign, not to them that believe, but to them that believe not' (1 Cor 14:22)—and it is quite clear from the book of Acts that this is so. We must test anything that claims to be a movement of the Spirit in terms of its evangelistic power.

This is important, because it is rather a subtle point. All the great movements of the Spirit as recorded in the Scriptures and in the subsequent history of the church, have always been great evangelistic movements. Revival, of course, always starts in the church but it does not stop there. God's way has been to revive his people and then, because they are revived, his power is manifested in their preaching, their witness, their testimony, and in the whole of their lives.

That is the characteristic of a true movement of the Spirit —it always has an outreach. On the other hand, the tendency of the counterfeit is to be a small, inward movement where you get a little coterie being formed, and where they just share wonderful experiences among themselves, but nobody else gets any benefit. This is, of course, always characteristic of the cults, which tend to be inward-looking with no outreach in that sense. But the great characteristic of the work of the Spirit is invariably this evangelistic consequence.

Watch the order. It must start in the church, which is then empowered to witness and testify boldly of the Lord. The Holy Spirit is not given that we may have wonderful experiences or marvellous sensations within us, or even to solve psychological and other problems for us. That is certainly a part of the work of the Spirit, but it is not the primary object. The primary object is that the Lord may be known. So you are entitled to judge anything that claims to be a movement of the Spirit—I am not here referring to an organized movement in connection with the Spirit or one concerned to teach about the Spirit—I am talking about a movement of the Spirit himself, the action of the Spirit. You are entitled to test that by applying to it this vital evangelistic test.

In other words, you see, such a movement of the Spirit is going to affect the whole church. It moves the whole church forward and does not merely gather together people who are interested in experiences and sensations and who are always turning round in a little circle. That is the cause of division. This is more general in its operation.

The next point I would emphasize is the one made by the Apostle when he says that these gifts are given in order that we may profit. 'The manifestation of the Spirit is given to every man to profit withal' (1 Cor 12:7). Now this again is a most important point. There is to be profit for the man himself and also for the whole church. Let me put it to you as you have it in 1 Corinthians 14:12—'Even so ye, forasmuch as ye are zealous of spiritual gifts, seek that ye may excel to the edifying of the church.' Now here is the great rule that the Apostle lays down: there must always be profit and edification. The moment we lose that again we have gone astray.

The devil, of course, will tempt us, as he has always tempted people throughout the centuries, to be interested merely in phenomena and experiences. We are all in the flesh, and we are all anxious to have certainty and assurance. The danger is that that may be turned inwards in such a way that we are only interested in sensation and experiences, and so forget the profiting; there are undoubtedly people, who go to meetings not that their minds may be enlightened or that they may be profited in their understanding, but because they want a thrill, they want to feel something.

Now this happens not only in connection with the doctrine of the baptism of the Spirit, it is also true of every church service. You will know full well of great rallies where some people just go from meeting to meeting waiting for some feeling, some thrill or excitement. They do not grow, they do not profit, nor do they increase in understanding, for they are not interested in those things. All they want is the excitement of the experience. The Apostle's teaching shows that this attitude is quite wrong. 'The manifestation of the Spirit is given to every man to profit withal', and it is to be always to the edifying of the church.

Now I come to the second heading, which again is a vitally important one—it concerns the way in which we seek the gifts. The Apostle says, 'Covet earnestly the best gifts' (1 Cor 12:31). It is at this point that the enemy once more tends to take advantage and to come in. Let us be clear about this; we are exhorted to seek the gifts and to desire them, and to do so earnestly. But here is where the danger enters. There are wrong ways of seeking the gifts. Well, let me note some of them.

First and foremost, of course, the spirit in which we seek them is vital in and of itself. If we seek these things with a selfish motive or merely with the desire to make ourselves important, so that we can speak and be prominent in giving testimony, rather than for the edification of the church, then we are already wrong.

We have to start by asking ourselves this first question—why do I desire these gifts? What is my motive and my object? And you will find that that will help you. Do you want it in order to have some thrilling and exciting experience? You are already wrong. The Holy Spirit is sent to glorify the Lord Jesus Christ and we must never forget that. Our motive should always be to know him so that we may minister to his glory and to his praise.

Having examined your motives, the second point I would make is this, and I do this in the light of some teaching that I have been reading recently. There is a teaching popular today which tells us that the quickest way of obtaining the baptism with the Holy Spirit is to get the gift of tongues which, they say, is very wonderful. If you want the baptism with the Spirit, start with tongues, and then that will probably lead you to the baptism with the Spirit. Now this is almost incredible because it cuts right across the whole of the teaching of the New Testament, which says that the gift of tongues is one of the manifestations of the Spirit. So you do not start with the tongues and go to the Spirit, you have the Spirit and the gift of tongues is one proof of it. But now the exact opposite is actually being taught. This is over-anxiety, of course, this is man coming in with his methods.

What does the New Testament describe? The apostles, and the hundred and twenty, met together in the upper room, the Holy Spirit came down upon them and they began to speak; they were first baptized with the Spirit, then began to speak in tongues. And so it is in all the other instances in Scripture. But the new teaching says start with tongues, it is the easiest and simplest way; and via tongues you arrive at the baptism of the Spirit. Well, there is no need to say more! It is just sheer lack of scriptural understanding, it is the flesh intruding and trying to do for us what the Spirit himself alone can do.

Let me put that still more plainly. There is nothing, it seems to me, so wrong and so dangerous as to try to induce or produce in ourselves the gifts of the Spirit. Again it is almost incredible that people should go astray on these matters. But people have always tended to do so and it is happening extensively at the present time. Their teaching is an attempt to help the Spirit to do his own work. Now Scripture teaches that the Holy Spirit is given to us, the risen Lord baptizes us with the Holy Spirit. 'The one upon whom thou shalt see the Spirit descending, and remaining on him', said God to John the Baptist, 'the same is he which baptizeth with the Holy Ghost.' And he alone does it, nobody else. He needs no assistance, the Spirit needs none of our help. The moment you try to help the Spirit you are already asking for trouble.

Take, for instance, a teaching which is well known at the

present time as to how one can be baptized with the Spirit. Here we are, Christian people, anxious to receive the best that God has to give us, and to receive the baptism with the Spirit in order that we may glorify the Lord and witness to him. We may feel we have not received this, so how do we do so? 'Quite simple,' we are told. 'Do you want the baptism of the Spirit? Well, all you need do is stay to an after meeting.' Then you sit on a chair and relax yourself as much as you can, relax your body. Then we are told that our Lord in the upper room 'breathed' the Holy Spirit upon the disciples and said, 'Receive ye the Holy Ghost'. So the next step in the teaching follows thus: 'Now remember he has breathed out the Holy Spirit; do you want to be baptized with the Holy Spirit? Well, this is all you have to do—in this relaxed condition, breathe in deeply, and as you are doing so you are breathing in the Holy Spirit into yourselves, and are receiving the baptism of the Holy Spirit. So relax and breathe in deeply and go on doing so, and as you are doing so you are breathing in the Holy Spirit.'

Now that is actually being taught! Where do you find anything approaching that in the New Testament? My dear friends, this is sheer psychological teaching and nothing but the power of suggestion. It is typical of the methods of psychology and you may have seen leading psychologists demonstrating on the television. And it is because Christian people teach this kind of thing that the critics are able to make their attacks while the world laughs in derision. But I am saying here that that teaching is not only unscriptural, it is purely carnal, not to say anything worse about it. Where do you see a man in the New Testament being told to relax and to breathe in deeply, or to do anything? No, what you find is that Christians are gathered together, praying to God, and suddenly he comes upon them; the household of Cornelius were sitting, listening to the preaching of Peter, and the Holy Spirit came upon them. In Ephesus Paul lays hands upon them and the gift is received; they do nothing by way of relaxing and deep breathing. That is psychology. And yet there are innocent people who follow this teaching and who fondly imagine that they have been baptized with the Spirit. They have not! They have either been hypnotized by another, or hypnotized themselves, or else they have entered into a state of hysteria; and, as I have already reminded you, psychological conditions can produce these phenomena as can spiritism. The moment you begin to do something like this in order to help the Spirit, you have already opened the most dangerous door you can ever open in your Christian life.

Let me give another illustration of the same thing. Take this question of speaking in tongues. When a man comes to me and tells me of some great occasion in his life when, while praying, the Holy Spirit suddenly came upon him and he was lifted up out of himself and found himself speaking in a strange tongue, I am ready to believe him and to accept him, especially if he tells me either that it has never happened to him again or that it has only happened very infrequently. I will accept it as being an authentic experience.

But when I read something like this (as I do so often in various journals) I am in an entirely different position. This is the teaching: 'Do you want to speak in tongues? 'Very well,' they say, 'this is what you have got to do; surrender your jaw and your tongue—let them go.' This is no laughing matter, my friends, the thing is too serious. There are people being led astray by such teaching today. 'Then,' they continue, 'then begin to utter sounds, any sort of sound, it doesn't matter whether it has sense or meaning or not; utter any sound that offers itself to you and go on doing that. And if you keep on doing it you will find yourself speaking in tongues.' And the simple answer is you probably will, but it will have nothing to do with the Holy Spirit. I do not hesitate to say that. Where is there any suggestion whatsoever that we have to do things like this in the New Testament? It is just not there at all. What happens in the New Testament is that a man is baptized with the Spirit and finds himself speaking in tongues. This is the gift of the Spirit and he is all-powerful. He does not need your help. But psychology does. If you want to be hypnotized, you have got to yield and surrender yourself, you have got to behave in an automatic manner, and do what you are told to do. That is exactly what these people are teaching.

Now I am not querying their motives; I know they are honest, and that their motives are good; what I am saying is that they are not only unscriptural, they are also putting themselves into the hands not only of the psychologists but perhaps even of evil spirits. You must do nothing at all. The Spirit gives these gifts 'severally to every man as he will'. That is the statement: 'All these worketh that one and the selfsame Spirit, dividing to every man severally as he will' (1 Cor 12:11). If I am going to give somebody a gift, I do not want any help from them. But that is what people are being taught to do at the present time, as if the Holy Spirit cannot decide, and cannot do it in and of himself. He does not need your help! The moment you begin to try to induce a gift you are acting psychologically; indeed, as I have said, you may be handing yourself over to evil spirits. That is exactly what happens to those who become 'mediums' in connection with such work; they just hand themselves over and they are used by evil spirits. There is nothing more dangerous than this, but what amazes me is how anybody who is a Christian can believe such teaching. Where is it, I ask, in the New Testament? It is not there at all! According to the New Testament it is the gift of the Spirit, it is in the sovereignty of the Spirit, and we must leave it entirely to him and do nothing ourselves in order to try to help or to induce it or to produce it.

I am expounding this to you in its extreme form because that is how it is being popularly taught today. There have been meetings in which they have tried to work up an excitement by clapping their hands or by repeating a chorus or a hymn. All that is pure psychology, and not needed. No! The way of the New Testament is the exact opposite; it is to go to him, to seek it of him. He is the giver. Do not do anything else. The Holy Spirit does not need our help, my friends, or our psychological aids. He does not need us to reduce the lights and to put up an illuminated cross over the pulpit. He does not need all our help with all our singing and all our preliminaries and working up of emotions.

I am not only speaking now, you see, about the baptism with the Spirit, I am thinking of popular evangelism also. If the Spirit is Lord—and he is—he does not need these helps, and anything that tries to help the Spirit to produce a result is a contradiction of New Testament teaching. 'Not with enticing words of man's wisdom', says the Apostle, 'but in demonstration of the Spirit and of power.' Go to him! Speak to him! Ask him! Pray to him! That is what they did in New Testament times, and that is what they have done in all the greatest and best periods in the subsequent history of the Christian church.

Let me end with this note. The best way of all, according to the apostle Paul, is the way that he outlines in 1 Corinthians 13. Look at that last verse in chapter 12: 'But covet earnestly the best gifts: and yet shew I unto you a more excellent way.' There is no passage of Scripture that has been more frequently abused and misinterpreted than just that. The common way in which the quenchers of the Spirit use it, of course, is this: 'Yet shew I unto you a more excellent way,' they say. 'Do not talk about or get interested in gifts; gifts are all right, but they are nothing. Go in for the graces.' They interpret it like that because they base their teaching upon the Authorized Version translation of that statement, which is incorrect. 'Yet shew I unto you a more excellent way', says the Authorized Version, but the translators had no right to translate it like that. There is no comparative at all in the original. The way it should be translated is: 'Moreover I show you an excellent way.' That is all. You might translate it like this: 'And yet I show you a way according to excellence.'

What does Paul mean by that? I agree with Charles Hodge when he interprets it like this: 'Covet earnestly the best gifts; and moreover I show you the way par excellence to obtain the gifts.' You see it is the exact opposite of those who say that this is to dismiss and to belittle the gifts. It cannot mean that because when the Apostle takes up the subject again at the beginning of chapter 14 he says, 'Follow after charity, and desire spiritual gifts.' He has not dismissed them, he is not contrasting the spiritual gifts with the graces. No, no, he says. If you really want the gifts, seek the graces. The best way to get the gifts is to seek the love of the Lord, his love to you and yours to him. If you are filled with this love then you are likely to get the best gifts. It is the way par excellence of obtaining them.

Without any question this is the New Testament way, as it has been the way of the saints throughout the centuries. Do not seek the gifts directly, seek them indirectly. Seek him! Seek his love! Seek his glory! Seek the knowledge of him! Seek the power to witness and to testify unto him! Be filled with a love to him and then you will get your gifts. If you do not, what will happen to you will be this. You may speak with the tongues of men and of angels, but because you have not got charity you will 'become as a sounding brass, or a tinkling cymbal'. Remember, that means that you will be able to speak in tongues but it will be of no value. 'And though I have the gift of prophecy, and understand all mysteries'—you have been seeking them directly—'and all knowledge; and though I have all faith, so that I could remove mountains, and have not charity, I am nothing.' It is no good.

In other words the prescription is—seek him! Seek his love, seek his life, seek to know him in the very vitals of your being; seek that you may be filled with love to him, and you will receive the gifts. Not talking about them always, not having meetings about them. No! Have meetings about him! Preach about him! Preach about him in the glory of his person and his divine saviourhood and all he has done. Preach him! Seek him! Love him! And he will give you the gifts to enable you to witness to him and to bear testimony to him and to the glory of his praise!

We must leave it at that, but these matters, as you can see, are of the most vital and urgent importance. Keep the balance, my dear friends. Keep your sense of proportion. And above all be wary lest in your anxiety to get gifts you may hand yourself over either to the psychologist or else to the evil spirits that are able to counterfeit even these choice and precious gifts of the Holy Spirit given by the risen Lord. May God give us all a spirit of understanding, and a spirit of wisdom with respect to these matters.

Chapter 8

Control of the Tongue

We have seen that Paul emphasizes above everything else that the purpose and the object of the gifts is to glorify the Lord. The Spirit himself has been sent to glorify the Lord Jesus, not to call attention to himself but always to point to the Lord. We must ever keep that in the forefront of our minds. We have seen too, that the next thing the Apostle takes up—and it is to this indeed that he gives most of his attention—is the whole question of balance and order. Finally, we considered briefly the way in which we seek these gifts. Paul tells us to 'Covet earnestly the best gifts', and we saw that there are certain false mechanical, psychological ways in which people can attempt to do this and so get themselves into trouble and ultimately bring the whole doctrine concerning gifts into disrepute.

We must continue to examine this whole question of gifts as the Apostle does. You notice that in 1 Corinthians 12-14 he gives the greatest prominence to the whole question of what is called 'speaking in tongues', because that was clearly the main cause of trouble in Corinth and the issue which was causing confusion. The object of the three chapters is really to put the question of speaking in tongues into its right place, to give the Corinthians a due sense of proportion with respect to it. They were putting it in the first place, talking about it and all trying to show that they possessed the gift. Thus the disorder to which he refers had entered into the life of the church.

There is no doubt whatsoever that this is the main object which the Apostle has in his mind, because he keeps on repeating it. The whole of the fourteenth chapter is virtually given over to this one thing, and it is interesting to notice the way in which he handles it. In the two lists he gives, he deliberately puts speaking in tongues last and he does this because the Corinthians were putting it first. That is his way of correcting them. And then he goes out of his way to repeat it several times, to show that prophecy is the greater gift and that this is the one they should seek. In other words, he deals with tongues by contrasting it with the gift of prophecy, thereby showing that the exaggerated importance which the Corinthians were giving to this speaking in tongues was entirely wrong.

We are dealing with it here because it is our duty to expound the Scriptures. If there is anybody who says at this point, 'I am not interested in the gift of tongues, or in 1 Corinthians 12-14', then I have to say to you that what I want to discuss with you is not the gift of tongues but your whole view of the Scriptures. Anyone who cuts out portions of Scripture is guilty of a very grievous sin. It is the business of all of us as Christians to understand the whole of the Bible, and unless we are making an effort to do so we are very poor Christians; quite apart from the fact that we are at the same time probably quenching the Spirit and are just desirous of going along in our undisturbed, self-satisfied, smug kind of formal Christianity. I have nothing to say to that except to warn such people that they will have to stand before God in the judgement and give an account of themselves, including how they have paid attention to the word that he has provided for them, and for their growth and development. That, then, is our main reason for considering it.

Another very good reason for considering this whole matter is that this question has received a great deal of prominence in this present century. A movement broke out in 1906, particularly in America, but also to some extent in this country, in connection with speaking in tongues. This movement has become known as Pentecostalism. We need not here go into the history of the movement but this subject has received a good deal of prominence ever since, and it behoves us, therefore, to know something about it. In recent years there has been a revival once more of interest in this, again starting mainly in America but also spreading to this and other countries. There is at the present time amongst many good, excellent Christian people a great deal of interest in the whole matter of speaking in tongues. It is, therefore, our business to be aware of the teaching of Scripture with respect to it in order that we may know what attitude to adopt.

Thirdly, and lastly, my reason for calling attention to this gift is that it is quite obviously, of all the spiritual gifts the one that is most likely to be misused and abused by believers. That is the whole thrust of this passage in 1 Corinthians. I do not know why this should be. It may be that it was the gift that was distributed most freely; it may well be because it is the least of the gifts. The trouble in Corinth was that they all wanted to speak in tongues and many of them wanted to do so at the same time. It tends to lend itself to exhibitionism and to promote selfishness.

Now the wonderful thing about the Christian life is that we are born again—but we are not made perfect. That is why we are liable to go astray, and to listen to the attacks of the enemy, the adversary of our souls. That is why these

New Testament letters ever came into being, because Christian people were being led astray in these various ways. And so I say there is no gift perhaps that is more liable to be abused than this one, none that is more liable to attract the carnal part of our being and so lead to excess and to abuse. And certainly it is true to say that there is no gift of the Spirit that has lent itself so much to the counterfeit of the devil in various forms than this particular gift.

I think I have already reminded you that it is quite possible for spiritists to speak in tongues—there is no question about that. There have been endless recorded cases of it. Not only that, people under certain psychological states and conditions can be made to do this under the influence of spiritists. I think of a certain lay pastor, who came to me in considerable distress over the case of a girl who was clearly devil-possessed and was able to speak in tongues. These things are well-established facts. Therefore I say, because of this, it behoves us to be unusually careful as we approach this subject. So we do so along the lines that I have already been indicating to you. We must avoid the two extremes, one of which is to dismiss the whole thing and refuse even to consider it.

I am amazed at some of the things I have read recently on the subject—certain Christian people have issued booklets and pamphlets, and in one of these the writer did not hesitate to say that 'all speaking in tongues today is of the devil'. How a man ventures to make such a statement I simply cannot understand. I would not dare to do so. No, we must be very careful in all we say and we must be open in this matter. The Apostle tells us, 'Wherefore, brethren, covet to prophesy, and forbid not to speak with tongues' (1 Cor 14:39). We have already dealt with the argument that says this belonged only to the early church. If you once go along that line you will soon find that the New Testament has practically nothing to say to you at all, you will have to say it was all for the early church. But clearly it was not, it is for us.

We start then by saying that it is always possible that the Holy Spirit may give this gift to certain individuals. So that when we hear of any reported case, we do not dismiss it, nor do we condemn it. We must examine it. In the sovereignty of the Spirit he can give any one of these gifts at any time; we must therefore be open. But for the reasons we have already adduced we must also always be cautious and careful, we must 'prove all things', and only 'hold fast to that which is good'.

Now what is the teaching in Scripture with regard to speaking in tongues? In the first place, speaking in tongues is not the invariable accompaniment of the baptism of the Spirit. I put it like that because there is teaching which has been current for a number of years and still is today, which says that speaking in tongues is always the initial evidence of the baptism with the Spirit. It therefore goes on to say that unless you have spoken in tongues you have not been baptized with the Holy Spirit. Now that, I suggest, is entirely wrong. In 1 Corinthians 12:30 the Apostle asks, 'Have all the gifts of healing? do all speak with tongues?' Again in 1 Corinthians 14:5 he says, 'I would that ye all spake with tongues, but rather that ye prophesied'. And when he says that he would that they all spake in tongues, he is clearly saying that they all did not. That, it seems to me, should be sufficient in and of itself.

But in addition to that there is other great evidence. When we were dealing with the question of the baptism with the Spirit in general* I gave you a number of quotations of some of the greatest and most saintly men the church has ever known, some of the greatest preachers and evangelists.

* See the companion volume *Joy Unspeakable* (ed.).

These were men who had received the baptism with the Holy Spirit after their conversion in a most unmistakable manner and who gave proof that they had received this by being used so mightily of God in evangelism and in revival; but none of them spoke in tongues, not one of them.

Now these are sheer facts and they surely should indicate to us how wrong it is to make these dogmatic assertions. But let me be quite fair; not all who belong to the Pentecostal church teach this: some do and some do not. It is very interesting to note that at the European Pentecostal Conference, which was held in Stockholm in 1939, it was admitted that tongues might occur apart from the Spirit's action. Now these men are honest men of God who were ready to admit in a world conference that powers other than the Holy Spirit can enable people to speak in tongues; they then went on to say that a Christian could be filled with the Spirit without the sign of tongues. Quite so ! They would have been flying in the face of the facts of history as well as in the plain teaching of the Scriptures had they not made that admission and concession.

Now I am concerned about all this for this reason. When people are told that unless they speak in tongues they have not been baptized with the Holy Spirit, many who have been baptized with the Holy Spirit are made to feel very unhappy. They say, 'But I have never spoken in tongues, and I am told that because of that, I have never been baptized with the Spirit.' But they had thought that they were, they had every reason for thinking that they were, and thus they are made unhappy.

But still more serious is the fact that having been made unhappy in this way by this false teaching, they then, of course, become much more open than they were before to psychological pressure, let alone the influence of evil spirits. They are so anxious to have this 'essential' evidence that they do everything they can to speak in tongues and, of course, after a while some of them begin to do so. But the question is—what has made them do so? Others remain unhappy and miserable, which is quite wrong and false. It is all due to this one teaching. It is to fly in the face of the Scriptures and the history of the church to say that unless a man has spoken in tongues, he has never been baptized with the Holy Spirit.

Let me say again that one of my main objects in this whole series of sermons is to safeguard the doctrine of the baptism with the Holy Spirit. There is a tendency on the part of some, because they dislike the gifts and the manifestations and the excesses, to throw out the doctrine of the baptism of the Spirit with it. Let me underline this important fact—you must differentiate between the two. It is possible for a man to be baptized with the Holy Spirit without ever speaking in tongues, and, indeed, without having some of these other gifts which the Apostle lists in this great passage that we are examining.

Let us come to the second matter. What is speaking in tongues? This is helpful again to throw light upon the present discussion. How do you define speaking in tongues? There is a difficulty that arises here because of what we are told in Acts 2 of what happened to the apostles and to those also who were gathered with them in that upper room on the day of Pentecost. We are told, 'And there appeared unto them cloven tongues like as of fire, and it sat upon each of them. And they were all filled with the Holy Ghost, and began to speak with other tongues, as the Spirit gave them utterance.'

Now the tendency in some is to identify that with what the apostle is speaking about in 1 Corinthians 12-14. And yet it seems to me that that is sheer confusion. I say that because it is perfectly clear from what happened on the day of

Pentecost that the apostles were speaking in known languages. We prove that by pointing out how the different people who were there were astonished that they were all hearing these men speaking in their own languages. 'They were all amazed and marvelled, saying one to another, Behold, are not all these which speak Galilæans? And how hear we every man in our own tongue, wherein we were born?' (Acts 2:7-8). They were clearly speaking in their languages.

There are some who say that what happened was that the apostles were speaking the normal language of Galilæans, but that the gift of understanding them was given to the other people. That is wrong for this reason: if that were so, it would be the other people on whom the Holy Spirit had descended. The miracle would have happened in the listeners. But the account tells us that the miracle had taken place in the speakers, in the apostles, who were enabled to speak these various languages, and the people were able to hear them. In other words, there was no need of an interpreter. The people knew the languages and they understood what was being said.

Now the whole point in 1 Corinthians 14 is that interpretation is an absolute necessity and that without interpretation the gift of tongues should not be exercised. There is this emphasis on the need for an interpreter in verses 2, 4, 14 and 15. It is clear to me, therefore, that in the Corinthian passage we are not dealing with 'known languages' as we were in Acts. There is a very good reason, which we need not go into here, why what happened on the day of Pentecost did happen. It is the answer to the Tower of Babel. It is the indication of the universality of the gospel.

But here we are dealing with something different. It is quite clear that in a cosmopolitan city, a seaport like Corinth, there would have been people from different parts speaking different languages. It is quite clear that if these Christians were speaking in various languages that there would have been people present who could have understood. The apostle Paul himself was a man who clearly could speak several languages, but he says that when he spoke in tongues there were times when he did not understand (see 1 Cor 14:14); as the gift of tongues was given so there was the gift of interpretation also. Therefore, it seems to me quite clear that in Corinthians we are not dealing with known languages. In any case there seems no point or purpose in a man in private prayer praying in some other known language. What is there to be gained by that? There does not seem to be any object or any purpose in it.

I want to suggest to you now that a lot of the trouble has arisen, because people have not given the full significance to the word 'tongue'—'in an unknown tongue' or 'in a tongue', the 'unknown' is generally supplied. What is the basic meaning of this word 'tongue'? Now I am not giving my own opinion here, but the opinion of the experts in these matters and there is no doubt but that the Greek word means 'speaking tongue', or if you prefer, 'the tongue in action'. It is not referring to dialects or languages.

What the Apostle is talking about here, therefore, is 'the tongue speaking as it is moved by the Holy Spirit'. Normally when a man speaks, his tongue moves as the result of his understanding and the direction of his will; but when a man speaks in a tongue, the tongue is in action as the result of the operation of the Spirit. All these gifts are gifts of the Spirit, and therefore the very word that is employed rejects this whole notion of languages or dialects, and is indicative of the fact that it is speech, the tongue in action, the tongue speaking as the result of the propulsion or direction or control of the Holy Spirit himself.

This seems to me to be made perfectly clear by the Apostle in verses 14 and 15 of chapter 14 where he says, 'If I pray in an unknown tongue, my spirit prayeth, but my understanding is unfruitful. What is it then? I will pray with the spirit, and I will pray with the understanding also: I will sing with the spirit, and I will sing with the understanding also.' You see the contrast is between 'praying in the spirit' and 'praying with the understanding'. In the one case it is the Spirit—the Holy Spirit—acting upon the man's spirit and moving his tongue. In the other it is the man himself with his understanding speaking through his tongue.

These are crucial verses and those who are familiar with Charles Hodge's commentary will know how he finds himself in considerable difficulty at this point. The only way in which he can get himself out of it is to say that what the Apostle is actually telling us is this: 'If I pray in an unknown tongue my spirit prayeth, but I am not giving understanding to other people.' But that is not what the Apostle says. Paul is talking about his own spirit and about his own understanding; not about giving understanding to other people. Indeed that is precisely what he is not saying, and that explanation, therefore, does violence to the whole text. There are other commentators who entirely agree with what I am saying. Paul is referring to something that happens in himself.

Verse 2 confirms this: 'He that speaketh in an unknown tongue speaketh not unto men, but unto God: for no man understandeth him; howbeit in the spirit he speaketh mysteries.' And he says in verse 4, 'He that speaketh in an unknown tongue edifieth himself'. This is the whole mystery with regard to this gift. It seems to me that we can only interpret it by saying that to speak in a tongue means that for the time being a man has been taken up by the Spirit. The Spirit has come upon him and has lifted him up into the spiritual realm and he finds himself speaking in a language that he does not understand. It is an extraordinary language. Though he does not understand it, it is yet edifying to him as verse 4 says. He does not understand the words but he knows what he is doing—he knows that he is glorifying God. That is the real meaning of verse 2: 'He that speaketh in an unknown tongue speaketh not for men, but for God.' It is better to translate it 'for' rather than 'unto'. He is not helping men as it were, he is not doing anything for men, but he is doing something for God. He is glorifying God, worshipping him, and magnifying him. He knows he is doing that, but he cannot identify the actual words that he is using. The whole thing is a mystery.

But, you see, we are dealing with the realm of the Spirit, a realm which is miraculous and which is supernatural. This is the theme which the Apostle has in mind throughout this whole chapter. These are *spiritual* gifts. This is not man's natural faculties being heightened; this is a gift, something new, something which is given. And so the Apostle says that what happens when a man speaks in tongues is that the Spirit is controlling him, by-passing his understanding for the time being. Instead of it coming through the understanding to the tongue, it goes directly through the man's spirit to the tongue.

The final proof of what I am saying is, of course, found when he contrasts tongues with prophesying. Prophesying means that a man again is enlightened by the Holy Spirit, but it is his understanding that is enlightened. So we read in the third verse, 'He that prophesieth speaketh unto men for edification, and exhortation, and comfort.' The operations of the Spirit are almost endless. The Spirit does enlighten a man's mind and his understanding. Thank God for this! We have all known this and preachers in particular know how the understanding can be heightened. But a man knows that it is coming through his understanding and the tongue is moved by the understanding enlightened by the Spirit. But in 'speaking in tongues' the understanding is not involved. It is something that happens directly through the Spirit acting upon the spirit of man moving the tongue.

Now I was very interested in turning up this definition in an excellent Lexicon by Arndt and Gingrich. They say that beyond any question at all the 'speaking in tongues' referred to in these chapters means 'broken speech of persons in religious ecstasy'. That is precisely what I am trying to say—that when a man speaks in tongues he is taken hold of, he is lifted up above himself and he speaks in a language that he does not understand. I am very ready to agree with those who say that he is probably speaking in the language of paradise, the language of the glory itself. I have always felt that this is similar to what we get in 2 Corinthians 12 where the Apostle says that, fourteen years before, he was lifted up into the heavens where he heard things that were inexpressible. I cannot prove this to you. But it seems to me to be the inevitable exposition here. So that this is not some kind of gibberish; it is a man possessed by the Spirit, lifted up into a condition of ecstasy in which he speaks in this language of glory, not understanding what he is saying, and yet knowing that it is the language of glory, and that he is glorifying God.

But let me add one qualification. Though I say that the man is in a state of religious ecstasy, it does not mean that he is unconscious; it does not mean that he has lost control of himself, as I will demonstrate to you later.

The next principle we come to is that speaking in tongues is not something that can be initiated by us. Or if you prefer it, a man cannot speak in tongues whenever he likes. Now this is to me perhaps the most important point of all. You will generally find with people who claim today to speak in tongues that most of them say that they can do so whenever they like. Ask them, 'Can you speak in tongues whenever you like?' They say, 'Yes, whenever we like', and they will do it for you there and then. I suggest that that puts them in a category outside the teaching of 1 Corinthians 14. This is to me one of the crucial points in the differentiation of true speaking in tongues from the counterfeit.

How do I substantiate this? I do so by calling attention to what the Apostle says in 1 Corinthians 14:18 where we read, 'I thank my God, I speak with tongues more than ye all.' Now that to me is a most crucial statement. Let us be careful to observe exactly what he does say. He does not say 'I speak with more tongues than you all.' I underline that because people who reject the whole of the supernatural and the miraculous in these chapters say that all the apostle Paul is claiming here is that he knew more foreign languages than the Corinthians did. They say the whole question refers to speaking in other languages and that the Apostle says 'Well, I happen to know more foreign languages than any of you.'

I reject that because it is wrong even grammatically. What he says is that he speaks more in tongues. It is an adverb; he means 'more frequently'. 'I thank my God, I speak in tongues more frequently than do you all.' Now if it is true to say that a man can speak in tongues whenever he likes, what is the point of the Apostle's statement? If it is true of all who have the gift of speaking in tongues that they can do so whenever they like at will—what is the point of the Apostle saying that he speaks in tongues 'more frequently' than they all do? It would simply mean that he decides to do so more frequently than they do. There is no purpose in saying that, and, indeed, in the next verse he makes such an explanation impossible for this reason: 'Yet in the church I had rather speak five words with my understanding, that by my voice I might teach others also, than ten thousand words in an unknown tongue.'

No, it seems to me that there is only one explanation of this statement which is that the Apostle is saying, 'I think I know more than any of you what it is to be taken up by the Spirit.' This is not something ordinary, but something remarkable, glorious and exceptional. He is saying, 'The Spirit comes more frequently upon me than any of you.' He tells them in effect, 'You are boasting, you are making me boast, and I am telling you that I know more frequently than any of you do what it is to have the Spirit taking hold of me and lifting me up into this realm.' It is the only conceivable explanation. Indeed, I suggest that verses 29 and 30 support this. He says, 'Let the prophets speak two or three, and let the other judge.' Then he goes on: 'If any thing be revealed to another that sitteth by, let the first hold his peace.' What does that mean? Well it means this. Suppose there is a prophet speaking; now, Paul says, if a message is given to another prophet, let the first stop in order that the second may speak. But you notice what it says, 'If a message is *given* to another prophet.' A prophet is not filled with messages which he can speak whenever he likes. No; the message is 'given'.

All the gifts are given. What applies to tongues applies also to miracles. Is there any evidence in the New Testament that a man who has the gift of miracles can work a miracle whenever he likes? Of course there is not. It is the exact opposite. It is the same with all these gifts. The prophet is not always filled with messages which he can turn on or give out whenever he likes. No, the message comes to him, it is given to him.

I think that this is the most important matter of all, because I suggest that if a man tells me that he can speak in tongues whenever he likes, it is probably something psychological and not spiritual. The spiritual gifts are always controlled by the Holy Spirit. They are given, and one does not know when they are going to be given.

Let me prove this to you by illustrating it in the case of miracles. Look at the apostles in Acts. They had the gift of miracles, but what is so interesting to observe is that the apostles never made experiments, or tried to heal somebody, wondering whether it would happen or not. No, there were no trials, no experiments and no failures. What is still more interesting is that the apostles never made an announcement that they would work miracles on such and such a day. They never put up a poster saying, 'Come on Thursday, there will be miracles performed'. Never! Why not? There is only one answer—they never knew when it was going to happen. What clearly happened was that they were suddenly confronted by a situation and the commission was given to them.

Take the first instance of this in Acts 3. We read that 'a certain man lame from his mother's womb was carried, whom they laid daily at the gate of the temple which is called Beautiful, to ask alms of them that entered into the temple; Who seeing Peter and John about to go into the temple asked an alms.' Then notice this: 'And Peter, fastening his eyes upon him with John, said . . . .' Now that is a clear indication that he was given a commission. This is not an experiment, he is not just trying to see what may happen. He knew. He said, 'Look on us. And he gave heed unto them, expecting to receive something of them. Then Peter said, Silver and gold have I none; but such as I have give I thee: In the name of Jesus Christ of Nazareth rise up and walk. And he took him by the right hand, and lifted him up: and immediately his feet and ankle bones received strength'. And Peter then turned to the gathered crowd and gave the explanation: 'The God of Abraham, and of Isaac, and of Jacob, the God of our fathers, hath glorified his Son Jesus . . . . and his name through faith in his name hath made this man strong, whom ye see and know.' In other words, Peter was clearly given this very definite commission, and so what he says happens.

You can find numerous examples of this. Take Acts 13 and the miracle that the apostle Paul worked upon the man Bar-

Jesus, who was with Sergius Paulus, a great man in the island of Paphos. We are told, 'But Elymas the sorcerer (for so is his name by interpretation) withstood them, seeking to turn away the deputy from the faith. Then Saul, (who also is called Paul,) filled with the Holy Ghost, set his eyes on him ...' This is not a man able to work miracles whenever he wants to. No, he is given a commission, and filled with the Holy Spirit, he says: 'O full of all subtilty and all mischief, thou child of the devil, thou enemy of all righteousness, wilt thou not cease to pervert the right ways of the Lord? And now, behold, the hand of the Lord is upon thee, and thou shalt be blind, not seeing the sun for a season.' The apostle Paul could not do that sort of thing whenever he wanted to; he is given a commission, and so what he says happens. It is absolutely certain.

It is the same with his healing of the man at Lystra in Acts 14:8 where you find the same expression again. 'The same heard Paul speak: who steadfastly beholding him, and perceiving that he had faith to be healed, Said with a loud voice ....' Can you not hear the authority? Can you not hear this note of commission? It is the Spirit who gives it. It is not a permanent possession in a man.

Then here is another striking example in Acts 16:16 in the case of the girl with a spirit of divination. 'And it came to pass, as we went to prayer, a certain damsel possessed with a spirit of divination met us, which brought her masters much gain by soothsaying: The same followed Paul and us, and cried, saying, These men are the servants of the most high God, which show unto us the way of salvation.' Now take note—'And this did she *many days*.' If the Apostle permanently had the power of exorcism, why did he not deal with her the first day? He knew it was a spirit of divination and that she was devil-possessed. He was not given his commission straightaway. 'This did she many days. But Paul, being grieved, turned and said to the spirit, I command thee in the name of Jesus Christ to come out of her.' He knew. There was no failure, there was no experimentation. Paul was given a commission and the evil spirit 'came out of her the same hour'.

I am saying all this to establish the fundamental point that what applies to miracles, exorcism and all the gifts applies equally to the gift of tongues. It is not something, therefore, that a man can do whenever he likes. No. 'I thank God that I speak with tongues more than ye all.' In other words, 'I know what it is', says the Apostle, 'to be dealt with by the Spirit in this matter more frequently than any of you.' He is not just saying, 'I decide to do this more often than any of you do.' No, that is not what he is saying—he says it happens to him. All these things are the gifts of the Spirit. They happen to us, they are given to us. And, therefore, I say that if we possess some gift which we can handle or use or employ whenever we like, it seems to me that that puts it out of the category of the spiritual gifts of 1 Corinthians 12-14. But it very definitely does put it into line with what we know about the realm of the psychological. Self hypnotism is something that one can do whenever one likes; that is its very characteristic.

I know a man, a missionary for years in China, who tells me that on one occasion when alone in his room, he was baptized with the Holy Spirit and found himself speaking in tongues. He has never done so since. Now he was often worried about this and spoke to me about it. I shall never forget his sense of release and of joy when I expounded 1 Corinthians 14:18 to him. I said, 'My dear friend, the fact that you tell me that it has only happened to you once makes me say that it was genuine and authentic. If you told me that you could do it whenever you liked I would be really troubled.' No, my friends, these things are spiritual gifts; they are in the control of the Holy Spirit, not in the control of man. They are gifts given to the church. He is the Lord, he gives to whom he will, he gives when he will. Let us therefore be very careful, lest we be deluded by the counterfeit in various shapes and forms. Consider again carefully the evidence of 1 Corinthians 14.

In order that I may conclude this, let me expand on what I said earlier that though the man who speaks in tongues is in a state of ecstasy he is still rational; he has not lost self-control. I prove that by 1 Corinthians 14:27-32. 'If any man speak in an unknown tongue, let it be by two, or at the most by three, and that by course; and let one interpret.' He could not say that if we were not able to control these things. 'But if there be no interpreter, let him keep silence in the church; and let him speak to himself, and to God.' You see, there is to be control. 'Let the prophets speak two or three, and let the other judge. If any thing be revealed to another that sitteth by, let the first hold his peace. For ye may all prophesy one by one, that all may learn, and all may be comforted.' Here is the crucial verse—verse 32: 'And the spirits of the prophets are subject to the prophets. For God is not the author of confusion, but of peace, as in all churches of the saints.'

So here is this marvellous and wonderful thing that though the Holy Spirit possesses us when he wills and lifts us up into this realm, yet we have not become irrational. You cannot initiate this, but you can control and stop it. That is the teaching of these chapters. It is the movement of the Spirit; yes, and he may come upon any number of people at the same time. But, the Apostle says, you are still rational and therefore there must be no confusion; there must be a limit to the number making public utterances and it must be done in order. Speaking generally of the church Paul says let it be prophecy rather than speaking in tongues. 'Wherefore, brethren, covet to prophesy, and forbid not to speak with tongues.'

But the teaching seems to be that you should exercise this gift, if you truly have it, on your own when you are in private prayer. The Apostle here is contrasting what happens in the church and what happens when you are in private. To make his meaning clear he takes a hypothetical case. He says, in effect, 'Imagine what the position would be if you all spoke in tongues at the same time.' Take verse 23: 'If therefore the whole church be come together into one place, and all speak with tongues, and there come in those that are unlearned, or unbelievers, will they not say that ye are mad?'

So here he clearly teaches this extraordinary thing that while he is lifted up into a realm even beyond understanding yet he retains perfect self-control. You will find in the counterfeit that self-control is often lost. You are encouraged to let yourself go and even to abandon your reason. You must not do that. We are never to put our minds out of action—never! If the Spirit chooses to do something directly to us above the understanding, well, praise God for it; but you must never surrender your understanding or 'let yourself go'. That is always to open the gate to false evil spirits, to the psychological, to suggestion, and to various other things. This is the glory of the way of the Holy Spirit—above understanding and yet the understanding can still be used. And so the Apostle can end his discourse by saying, 'Let all things be done decently and in order.' A prophet cannot initiate, but he can control: 'The spirits of the prophets are subject to the prophets.'

May God grant that we may meditate more and more upon this great teaching of the baptism with the Holy Spirit and his gifts so that we may be able to discriminate and to differentiate in these days in which we live. 'Prove all things; hold fast that which is good.'

Scripture Index